# *Training for Transformation*

## *Book  II*

# Training for Transformation

## A handbook for community workers

## Book II

ANNE HOPE
and
SALLY TIMMEL

*Illustrations by Chris Hodzi*

PRACTICAL ACTION
Publishing

Practical Action Publishing Ltd
Schumacher Centre for Technology and Development
Bourton on Dunsmore, Rugby,
Warwickshire CV23 9QZ, UK
www.practicalactionpublishing.org

First published in 1984
Revised 1995
Reprinted 1999, 2000, 2001, 2003, 2005, 2007, 2009

Sold only as part of a three-book pack:
ISBN 978 1 85339 353 2

A catalogue record for this book is available from the British Library.

Since 1974, Practical Action Publishing (formerly Intermediate Technology Publications
and ITDG Publishing) has published and disseminated books and information in support of
international development work throughout the world. Practical Action Publishing Ltd
(Company Reg. No. 1159018) is the wholly owned publishing company of Practical Action Ltd.
Practical Action Publishing trades only in support of its parent charity objectives and any
profits are covenanted back to Practical Action (Charity Reg. No. 247257,
Group VAT Registration No. 880 9924 76).

Typeset by J&L Composition Ltd, Filey
Printed by Replika Press Pvt. Ltd

# Preface

All the theories, codes and exercises in this book have been used effectively with groups in Africa since 1975. Most of the examples and quotations in these books come directly from our experience, which has been mainly working with church-sponsored groups in Africa. There is therefore an African and a Christian perspective throughout.

For us, the spiritual dimension was lif-giving, and constantly challenged us to reach beyond the daily struggle. We believe the spiritual dimension is essential in the process of breaking through the apathy and discouragement, even hopelessness, which groups often experience as they try to face the hard facts of reality and engage in social analysis.

It will be necessary for all teams using the books to adapt the approach to their own cultural context, to find examples, stories, proverbs from the life of local people and to seek out those texts from the religious tradition(s) of the community which reinforce the vision of transformation towards a just, peaceful and happy society. These texts are to be found in all the great religions and in the literature of liberation struggles, and socialist and environmental movements.

Since the books were first published in 1984, there have been vast, unpredictable changes in the world. On the global political level, it seems the world will never be the same. Yet very little has changed for the vast majority of poor people in the South or so-called 'Third World'. (We prefer to call the "Third World" the Two-thirds World because two-thirds of the world's people belong to it.) In some places life has become more and more difficult.

We felt it was important for us to rethink our analysis of the causes of global poverty and our understanding of hopeful guidelines towards solutions. There is much talk of participatory democracy nowadays, but few training programmes for leaders to help them ensure authentic participation at the grassroots level. This is exactly what those using **Training for Transformation** have appreciated most about these books.

We are convinced that the fundamental approach, which lies at the core of the books, is as relevant and needed as ever. We have added new insights, theories and exercises which have enriched our own practice in recent years.

There is no short cut to effective leadership of groups. Sensitivity to the needs of the group and quick sure judgements on what will be most helpful at any particular moment, can only be developed through constant practice, complete openness to feedback from participants, critical reflection, analysis, and years of experience.

This set has been produced in three books mainly because it is easier to use this in the field than one large, bulky book. Each book belongs with the other two.

**Book one** is basically the theory of Paulo Freire on developing critical awareness and how to put this theory into practice.

**Book two** is focussed on the skills necessary for participatory education. To break the "culture of silence", people need to gain a sense of self-confidence and know that what they think is important. Therefore methods to involve the group actively are critical in group leadership, as are ways of clarifying and implementing the goals of the group.

**Book three** deals with the social analysis necessary to develop critical awareness and long-term planning and with steps needed for building solidarity in people's movements.

The set is written mainly for practitioners. It shows how to put basic theory into practise. It is also written to provide educators and community workers with some tools to help people to shape their own lives.

> **"Reflection without action is mere verbalism.**
> **Action without reflection is pure activism."**

The books try to combine both reflection and action in a clear and simple way. The following is a summary of the content of each chapter. A detailed table of contents of each book is found at the beginning of that book.

— Anne Hope and Sally Timmel
March, 1994

**Book I** deals mainly with helping local communities identify the issues which trouble them most, and on which they would like to work for change. We cannot hope to achieve real participation at grassroots level unless we start with the issues the people are really concerned about.

> **Chapter 1** deals with Paulo Freire's approach to transformation.
> **Chapter 2** explains how to do a survey in a community to find these issues.
> **Chapter 3** explains how to make good posters, plays and other problem-posting materials, which will help a group focus on a particular problem and go through the necessary steps, leading from reflection to action.
> **Chapter 4** is a summary of how to use this approach in a literacy program.

**Book II** deals with group leadership skills and group dynamics (forces and feelings that play a role in any group). Without an understanding of these, one cannot ensure participation.

> **Chapter 5** has theories and exercises for creating the conditions necessary for developing a spirit of trust, and an atmosphere in which true dialogue can take place.

> **Chapter 6** deals with different styles of leadership and their effect on participation.

> **Chapter 7** deals with steps in making decisions and planning action.

> **Chapter 8** is about evaluation. This should be a process of growth for all taking part, not simply a judgement from an outsider.

**Book III** moves from the local level to the wider context. It provides tools for analysing how forces operating at national and international levels affect local efforts towards development.

> **Chapter 9** provides a short history of the development decades and some useful tools of analysis, including an exercise challenging people to envision a new society. We find it essential to challenge a group to express their vision of the society they long for, as this develops energy and hope.

> **Chapter 10** uses the "parabola model" (based on following a Guiding Star) to outline the steps in building a people's movement.

**Chapter 11** recognises that vision is not enough. To bring about change effectively, one must also have good administration and management. However, this does not necessarily mean the hierarchical, top-down structures to which most of us are accustomed. We have to create new forms of management which are consistent with the beliefs and values of democratic participation.

**Chapter 12** is about planning workshops. The opportunity to spend time together, especially to stay together overnight for a weekend or several days, is very precious. It can be a time of grace, new vision, new energy. But people are so busy that such opportunities are rare and the time must be well used. Good workshops do not just happen, they must be carefully designed. A good workshop is a work of art. It takes time and experience to learn how to prepare them well. This chapter gives guidelines for designing workshops and some spiritual and theological background.

## HOW TO USE THESE BOOKS

If you have not participated in a DELTA training program, begin by reading Chapter 1 of these books. This will explain the approach used in these books. Then return to the Table of Contents and get an overview of the books as a whole.

It is tempting to dip immediately into the sections in Book II, on the needs which one already experiences in group work. Many people have used the books only in this way. This will certainly help improve the quality of participation and satisfaction with meetings. However, if one really wants to generate new energy and creativity in the process of development and employment, it is necessary to use all three books. We have found that a dynamic process occurs when integrating all of the elements of the three books. A piecemeal approach of just one element or the other does not have the same impact.

These methods can assist a community to start a process of reflecting on their issues, analysing the causes of their problems, so that local groups and then a regional development movement can be built. However, local problems are profoundly affected by forces on the national and international level. Local efforts at development will be ineffectual unless these are taken into account. We strongly recommend the use of some of the tools of analysis and processes of building a movement described in Book III.

1. **Read** the books.

2. **Study** the theories in each chapter.

3. **Test out** new exercises with a group you know well or with friends, and then write down the necessary adaptations for your situation.

4. **Try new exercises** each time you run a workshop. This can help prevent one from becoming stale by repeating the exercises you know well over and over again. If you feel shy about this, ask the group if they are willing to try out something new with you. This can take some of the pressure off and they can decide if it is a helpful tool. This also gives you confidence and a sense of creativity in trying out new activities.

5. **Take time to prepare** the new exercise or design. Some of these are not always easy processes. Take time before workshops to prepare, so you feel more at ease during a workshop.

# TABLE OF CONTENTS

## Book I

### Chapter 1.  Roots of this method
Introduction .................................................................................................. 3
Purpose of these books ................................................................................. 9
The five streams that form the DELTA River .............................................. 14
Paulo Freire's work on critical awareness .................................................... 14
Human relations training ............................................................................... 29
Organisational development .......................................................................... 30
Social analysis ............................................................................................... 31
Christian concept of transformation ............................................................. 33

### Chapter 2.  Survey for generative themes
Survey of community themes ........................................................................ 53
Survey method .............................................................................................. 54
Critical analysis of themes ............................................................................ 59
From the survey to codes and discussion outlines ....................................... 63
Surveys for workshops ................................................................................. 67

### Chapter 3.  Problem-posing materials
Making codes and discussion outlines .......................................................... 75
Preparation of codes ..................................................................................... 76
Digging deeply in discussion ........................................................................ 78
Codes and exercises on: ............................................................................... 83
    Development ............................................................................................ 83
    Approaches to basic needs ....................................................................... 86
    Wheel of fundamental human needs ........................................................ 86
    Identifying some root causes .................................................................... 102
    Practical projects: A beginning, not an end .............................................. 112
Development is the new name for peace ....................................................... 120

### Chapter 4.  Adult learning and literacy training
Adult learning ............................................................................................... 127
Process of learning ........................................................................................ 128
How adults learn ........................................................................................... 130
Education for what? ...................................................................................... 132
Literacy and development ............................................................................. 134
A demonstration of literacy class ., .............................................................. 138
How does it feel to be illiterate? ................................................................... 139
A guide for developing a literacy program ................................................... 144

### Resources
Poetry, readings and prayers ........................................................................ 150
Films .............................................................................................................. 166
Simulations .................................................................................................... 173
Bibliography .................................................................................................. 173

## Book II

### Chapter 5:  Trust and dialogue in groups
Groups skills needed for conscientization .................................................... 4
Developing trust in a group ........................................................................... 6
The learning climate ...................................................................................... 9
Introduction exercises ................................................................................... 18
Listening exercises ........................................................................................ 27
Trust building exercises ................................................................................ 36

**Chapter 6.  Leadership and Participation**
Leadership ....................................................................49
Content and process ......................................................53
Shared leadership .........................................................59
Self and mutual criticism..............................................65
Exercises on co-operation ............................................82
The group as the place of forgiveness

**Chapter 7.  Simple decision-making and action planning.**
Decision-making exercises and theories ........................95
Action planning ...........................................................104
Exercise on how to organise a workshop ......................111
The planning kit...........................................................114

**Chapter 8.  Evaluation**
Participatory evaluation ................................................122
Evaluation exercises for workshops ..............................131

# Book  III

**Chapter 9.  Tools of analysis**
Introduction ..............................................................3
Shape of the World ....................................................4
A.  The Evolution of Global Thought on Development.................8
B.  Alternat ives for a New Society .....................................31
C.  National/Local Tools of Analysis ..................................41
  1.  Simple Economic Tools ...........................................43
  2.  Political Analysis ..................................................57
  3.  Culture, Values and Beliefs .....................................66
  4.  Four Responses to Poverty ......................................75
  5.  Levels of Awareness...............................................80

**Chapter 10.  Building a movement**
Goals. The parabola model ..........................................85
Values and assumptions................................................94
Setting goals................................................................111
Planning ......................................................................112
Roles ...........................................................................118
Relationships ...............................................................127

**Chapter 11. New forms of management and supervision**
Theory X and Theory Y................................................136
What could be a new model of management....................142
Administration and management codes and exercises ......147
Codes and exercises for supervision ..............................161

**Chapter 12.  Planning workshops**
Carrying out a workshop ..............................................175
Possible designs for workshops .....................................180
DELTA  program of Training of trainers ........................184
Linking Development with Spiritual practice ..................186
Definition of terms ......................................................197

Index....................................................................200

# Book II:  Table of contents

**Chapter 5.  Preparing for participation:**
**Trust and dialogue in groups**

    **A.  Groups skills needed for conscientization** ........ 4
    **B.  Developing  trust in a group** ........................... 6
    **C.  The learning climate** ..................................... 9
    1.  Room arrangement ..................................... 9
    2.  Size of group ............................................ 10
    3.  Groupings for different purposes ..................... 14
    4.  Timing and pacing ..................................... 15
    5.  Brainstorming .......................................... 15
    6.  Use of newsprint ...................................... 16

    **D.  Introduction Exercises** .................................. 18
    1.  Gesture ................................................... 18
    2.  Stand Up If .............................................. 18
    3.  Brainstorming and Interviews ....................... 20
    4.  Drawings ................................................ 21
    5.  The Pie ................................................... 21
    6.  The journey of my life ................................ 22
    7.  Photo language ......................................... 23
    8.  Introductions on the move ........................... 24
    9.  Group introductions ................................... 25
    10.  Most important events ................................ 26

    **Listening Exercises** ........................................ 27
    1.  Dialogue or monologue ............................... 27
    2.  Listening in silence .................................... 27
    3.  Listening in pairs ...................................... 27
    4.  Input on listening techniques ....................... 29

    **Trust building exercises** ................................... 36
    1.  Past—present—future ................................ 36
    2.  7—12 years old ........................................ 36
    3.  River of Life ........................................... 37
    4.  Tree of Life ............................................ 38
    5.  Class origin — Class option ......................... 39
    6.  Potato exercise ......................................... 41
    7.  Building unity across age, race,
        tribe and sex ........................................... 42

**Chapter 6.  Leadership and Participation** .................. 47
    **A.  Leadership** ................................................ 49
    **B.  Content and process** ................................... 53
    1.  What to observe in a group .......................... 53
    2.  Sociogram .............................................. 54
    3.  Role play on different leadership styles ........... 56
    **C.  Shared Leadership** ..................................... 59
    1.  PO-PO ................................................... 61
    2.  Drawing a house ....................................... 62
    3.  Mirroring ................................................ 62
    4.  Participation Open ..................................... 63
    5.  Methods Used .......................................... 63

    **D.  Self and Mutual criticism** .............................. 65
    1.  Johari's window ....................................... 65
    2.  Multiple role exercise ................................. 68
    3.  Strengthening  team relations ....................... 69
    4.  Team effectiveness  questionnaires ................. 70
    5.  Unhelpful behaviour — Animals ................... 73
    6.  Parent/Adult/Child ................................... 77

    **E.  Exercises on Co-operation** ............................ 82
    1.  Jigsaw cow .............................................. 82
    2.  Build with what you've got .......................... 83
    3.  Co-operative squares exercise ...................... 84
    4.  Competition or co-operation? ....................... 87
    **F.  Group reacton to the animator** ..................... 89

**Chapter 7.  Simple Decision-making and**
            **Action  planning** ............................... 97
    **A.  Simple Decision-Making** ............................. 95
    Decision-making exercise ................................. 95
    Theory 1.  Involvement in decisions ................... 96
    Theory 2.  Difficulties in decision-making ........... 98
    Theory 3.  Making good decisions ..................... 101
    4.  A simple guide for making
        decision by consensus ................................ 102
    5.  Who should make which decisions ................. 102
    6.  Factors which help decision-making .............. 103
    **B.  Action Planning** ........................................ 104
    1.  Mapping the situation ................................ 104
    2.  7 steps of planning ................................... 105
    3.  The 3  C's .............................................. 105
    4.  Force field analysis .................................. 108
    5.  PERT .................................................... 109
    6.  Exercise on how to organise
        a workshop ............................................ 111
    7.  The planning kit ...................................... 114

**Chapter 8.  Evaluation** ....................................... 121
    **A.  Participatory Evaluation** ............................. 122
    1.  What is evaluation .................................... 122
    2.  Evaluation exercise ................................... 123
    3.  Why do we evaluate? ................................ 123
    4.  Problems exercise .................................... 124
    5.  When do we evaluate? ............................... 125
    6.  Ethics of evaluation .................................. 125
    7.  Planning questions and indicators ................. 125
    8.  Methods of evaluation ............................... 126
    9.  Historical reflection .................................. 127
    10.  Planning the program for
        participatory evaluation .............................. 130
    **B.  Evaluation Exercises for Workshops** ........... 131

# Chapter 5

## Preparing for participation:
## trust and dialogue in groups

**This chapter includes:**

A. Group skills needed for conscientisation ...................................................4
B. Developing trust in a group ...................................................................6
C. The learning climate ............................................................................9
D. Introduction exercises .........................................................................18
E. Listening exercises .............................................................................27
F. Trust building exercises .......................................................................36

# Chapter 5

# Preparing for participation: trust and dialogue in groups

**A visit to a village in Maharashtra, India, with the Shramik Sanghatana or 'Toilers' Union**

"If the collective spirit of the people was impressive, it was the women and young girls who seemed to embody it the most, as they sang sitting in huts or marching through the village. They were more free and spirited, more collective in their singing . . . [they were singing] songs of struggle . . . And they sang of the 'new wave' that had come to the villages . . . and [through their organising] drunkenness had diminished, husbands were not beating wives so much, and it began to appear that although 'war is unhealthy for children and other growing things', class struggle on the contrary is healthy!

"Behind this activity of the women, an interesting process was going on. The activities from the beginning had worked to build up local leadership, to give some kind of political education; defeating the landlords meant also changing the social and political consciousness of the people and replacing a traditionalist, accommodating leadership of tribal elders by militants from among the youth."

*We Will Smash this Prison! Indian Women in Struggle*
Gail Omvedt
Zed Press, London, 1979
page 93

Building trust and dialogue in society cannot be done by pronouncements nor by some "magical waving of a wand". Dialogue begins at the local level, in small units and thus in groups.

Participation of people in shaping their own lives and writing their own history means enabling them **to speak own words – not the words of someone else.**

Sharing information should not be confused with participation. Mass meetings where information about new legislation, government policies, etc., is passed on, are necessary but they are not the same as participation of people. It is a more personal form of mass communication than radio or television, but is not participation. Nor is it true participation when people listen to the commands of those in authority, and then submissively do the "donkey work" involved.

Participation means dialogue. Dialogue is based on people sharing their own perceptions of a problem, offering their opinions and ideas, and having the opportunity to make decisions or recommendations.

As Paulo Freire has said, the issues facing a people are often complex and no expert has all the answers. On the other hand, nobody is totally ignorant. Each person has different perceptions based on his or her own experience. To discover valid solutions, everyone needs to be both a learner and a teacher. It is a mutual learning process.

# A.   Group skills needed for conscientisation

**To break the culture of silence**, people need to gain a sense of self-confidence and know that what they think is important. This does not happen quickly. It is a matter of practice for the participants and requires genuine belief in the animator that people can contribute to the transformation of society.

Because of the roles people have taken on, both in traditional culture and in the colonial, capitalist, and bureaucratic socialist states, there has been very little practice in democracy. Only the prescribed leaders have full voice in the shaping of the future. Nowadays the experts, and top managers, or the "educated" shape the nation. If people are suddenly asked to participate in a development project, they are either suspicious or expect that the leader is using them for their own ends. In fact, **the people are right to be suspicious!**

Frantz Fanon in his book *The Wretched of the Earth** gives many accounts of how the Western educated leaders, during the struggle for independence, and especially after independence, refused to be in dialogue with the people. At both moments, the "educated" had the opportunity to develop programs and long-term objectives with the rural population, but they stayed isolated in their urban settings. A great mistrust built up in the rural people. At the same time the traditional feudal leaders, as Fanon calls the chiefs, saw the threat posed by the Western educated, and thus the battle for power and authority not only began, but continues today. With the massive migration of the poor to cities during the last few decades, the division is now between the elite and both the rural and urban poor.

Power in itself is not a bad thing. All human beings have energy and some measure of power, unless it has been taken away from them. But domination and oppression, the pattern of "power over" people, must be broken. It should be replaced by "power with," that is, shared power.

People everywhere have been reacting against domination in huge impersonal states, for example in the break-up of the Soviet Union. It seems as if people are seeking smaller-scale national units, where it is possible to keep a sense of the whole in one's head and one's heart, and share in the making of responsible decisions. We see group methods of ensuring authentic participation as a means towards transformation. We realise that these methods can also be used to dominate and manipulate others, and we need to be constantly on guard that we are using them in a way that genuinely enables people to grow in awareness, maturity and self-reliance and not to control them.

**Group methods are meant to help structure our work time together so that we can learn better ways of uniting our efforts towards the transformation of this world.**

Group leadership training can be used to help people become sensitive to how others see them and more realistic about how one sees oneself. For some people, this has become an end in itself, ignoring the need for justice in the wider society. But self-knowledge needs to be seen in relation to the community and our role in it.

---

Fanon, Frantz, *The Wretched of the Earth*, Penguin Books Ltd. Great Britain, 1963, pp. 83 –98.

> ### Dialogue requires faith
>
> "Dialogue also requires an intense faith in human beings; their power to make and remake, to create and recreate; faith that the vocation to be fully human is the birthright of all people, not the privilege of an elite.
>
> Founded on love, humility and faith, dialogue becomes a horizontal relationship of mutual trust. Trust is established by dialogue; it cannot exist unless the words of both parties coincide with their actions.
>
> Nor can dialogue exist without hope. Hope is rooted in our human incompleteness, from which we move out in constant search, a search which can be carried out only in communion with other people. As long as I fight, then I am moved by hope, and if I fight with hope, then I can wait.
>
> Finally, true dialogue cannot exist unless it involves critical thinking, thinking which sees reality as a process, in transformation, thinking which does not separate itself from action but constantly involves itself in the real struggle without fear of the risks involved."
>
> Paulo Freire
> *Pedagogy of the Oppressed,* p. 62

Methods are not neutral, just as content is not neutral. If we believe that the participation of people is essential in the transformation of society, then our methods must be consistent with our aim: that is participatory education. If we also believe that people need to be involved in transformative action which breaks the structures of domination, then the methods we use must enable people to unveil the values and structures which dominate them.

## B.   Developing Trust in a Group

In any workshop, seminar or meeting, we need to be constantly sensitive to group needs. We cannot emphasise often enough that building trust, openness and honesty between people is a critical element for community action. This demands great openness on our part, not only for others. As animators, we need to be open to feedback about the way we work and to take time to examine our own values, attitudes and beliefs. Being an animator means continuous learning.

This is also true for groups. Trust is never finally achieved. Even if members of a group have known each other well, the process of trust building is continuous.

---

**No matter how full the river, it still wants to grow**

– Congo

---

Jack Gibb recognised that all groups have four needs if they are to grow in mutual trust:*

   a.   **Acceptance.**
   b.   **Sharing information and concerns.**
   c.   **Setting goals.**
   d.   **Organising for action.**

### Acceptance

From the beginning, people need assurance that they are truly accepted as they are – that it is safe to say in the group what they really think and feel. The uniqueness of each person, with his/her own experience and insights, needs to be recognised. People, like plants, need the right kind of "climate"  to grow, and the animator has a special role and responsibility in developing such a "climate"  in the group. It is essential if the group is to grow into a real community.

Unless there is this spirit of respect and acceptance, people will not be free to learn, to re-think their old opinions, to share fully their thoughts and feelings.

---

\* Jack Gibb writes also about building a learning group. See *Basic Reading in Human Relations Training,* Book 1, Episcopal Church, p.23.

## Sharing information and concerns

People working in groups need information:
- about each other; their experience, their ideas, their values and opinions
- about the issues which they consider to be important in their lives.

They need to work out for themselves what they need to know. Information poured out randomly on a group is likely to bore them unless they see the relevance to their own lives.

The animator also needs an opportunity to share his/her concerns and information, but this should be done after other members of the group have shared theirs, and this should also be offered for discussion, not imposed on the group.

Very often the concern of the animator and those who arranged the meeting will be to help people deepen their awareness, to move from the symptoms to the causes of the problem. The Problem-Posing Method is a particularly effective way of doing this.

## Setting goals

The third need of a group, recognised by Gibb, is to set goals clearly. Unless the goals are set by the group, people will not be interested in or committed to carrying them out. Unless the goals are clear to all, people become frustrated. The way decisions are made is directly related to how committed people feel to carrying them out. (See Chapter 10.)

## Organising for action

Once goals have been set, the group needs to make definite plans to reach these goals and carry out decisions. Definite people need to take responsibility to do definite things, and they should be accountable to the group to get these things done. This is why they need to accept these responsibilities publicly where possible. This implies the need for a structure which is appropriate for the group and which will ensure that one person will not assume all the responsibility or control all the actions.

It is essential to check how participants feel about a meeting and the plans made. An **evaluation** is needed immediately after a group meeting, and again some time later, to make sure that plans are working effectively and that all are carrying out their responsibilities. This second evaluation should be planned before the first meeting finishes.

These four needs should usually be met in this order in a meeting or workshop, but Gibb points out that often they are not settled once and for all. Any one of these needs can occur again at any point in the meeting, and the best animators are those who are sensitive enough to recognise the need and find a way of meeting it. These four points of Gibb's Theory of Trust can also be used as the framework within which one plans the different sections of a workshop. (See section on planning Workshops, Chapter 12. )

## The importance of team training

The participation of people in teams, rather than as isolated individuals, is critical for building trust, accountability and effective action.

## Discussion questions

1. How often have we seen groups work in Gibb's way?

2. How often do they work backwards: i.e. start with a structure, then try to define their goals, then realise they need more information to form goals, and finally recognise interpersonal difficulties because they do not know each other? Give examples.

3. Do you think Gibb's theory is correct? Why or why not?

4. What can we do in our own groups to follow these guidelines of Gibb's?

## Some guidelines for trust building*

Some simple guidelines for trust building and listening in a group.

**Ground rules**

1. Patience, don't jump on anyone else
2. Everyone has the right to express their responses and opinions in the time available
3. Only one person speaks at a time
4. Everyone has the right not to speak
5. No "killer statements" that put down other people
6. No self put-downs
7. Changing one's mind can be a sign of growth

*Adapted from Sid Simon, *Helping Your Child*, pp. 43-45

# C.  The Learning Climate

## 1.  ROOM ARRANGEMENT

Research has shown that the arrangement of a room has a strong effect on participation in a discussion. Those who can see all the other faces are at an advantage and those who cannot are at a disadvantage. If people are sitting in straight rows, it is very unlikely that a good discussion will develop between them because they cannot see one another's faces. Most questions and comments will be directed to those facing the group.

Every effort should be made to enable the participants to sit in one circle where everyone can see everyone else's face. If the circle becomes so big that people cannot hear each other, it is better to have two concentric circles (or horseshoes, if they need to see something on the wall).

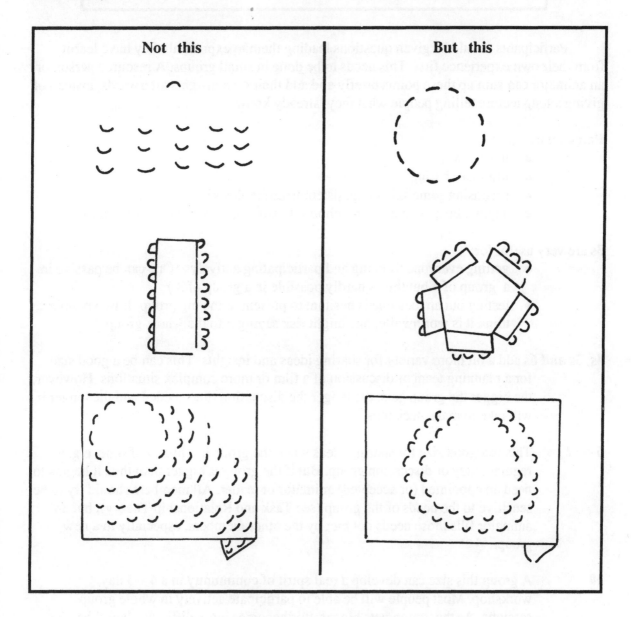

## 2.    SIZE OF GROUPS

The majority of people find it difficult to speak in a big group of strangers. Also there is usually not enough time for everyone to speak. Therefore if everyone is to participate actively, small groups are essential.

The majority of people find it difficult to listen very attentively for long periods. Therefore talks should be short and people should be given an opportunity to discuss in small groups the points made.

> **We all remember much better what we have discovered and said ourselves than what others have told us.**

Participants should be given questions leading them to express all they have learnt from their own experience first. This needs to be done in small groups. A resource person or an animator can sum up these points briefly and add their own insights afterwards, instead of giving a long lecture telling people what they already know.

**Pairs** are useful for:
- interviews,
- intimate sharing,
- practising some skills (e.g. listening or feedback)
- a quick buzz with one's neighbour to stir a passive, sleepy group into action.

**3s** are very useful for:
- getting everyone thinking and participating actively . (One can be passive in a group of 5 but this is hardly possible in a group of 3.)
- testing out an idea one is hesitant to present to the big group. If two people think it is worthwhile, one might risk saying it to the whole group.

**4s, 5s and 6s** add a bit more variety for sharing ideas and insights. This can be a good size for a planning team or discussion of a film or more complex situations. However, the bigger the group gets, the longer the discussion time needed and the longer it will take to make decisions.

**6 – 12**    This is a good size for sharing ideas when the group has plenty of time, e.g. a regular study or discussion group. But if the group is bigger than this, it begins to need an appointed (or accepted) animator or leader. All members should try to be sensitive to the needs of the group (see Task and Relationship Theory), but an animator fills those needs not met by the other members, especially in a new group.

**30**    A group this size can develop a real spirit of community in a 4 – 5 day workshop. Most people will be able to participate actively in whole group sessions. As the group gets bigger, this becomes more difficult. It will be necessary with groups this size to break into smaller groups of different kinds for different purposes.

> **Rule of Thumb.** The bigger a group is, the more skillful leadership and definite structure it needs in order to enable everyone to contribute freely and feel satisfaction in the meeting.

**30 – 200** (or 2000). Such groups can be useful to bring people into contact with new ideas, plan policy for big organisations, etc. However, if 98% of the group are not to be passive, they need very skillful facilitators and a team of trained animators to lead small discussions and feed ideas into the planning for the big group. It is often helpful to have one animator for each small group, trained ahead of time. These animators could meet 2 or 3 days before a conference for training.

If such conferences are to bring about any real changes they should not be completely filled with lectures followed by questions and answers. Time must be provided for participants to understand the new ideas by discussing them in small groups, and to plan how they will implement them with people working in the same or similar situations. If this is not done at the conference, even if people are convinced by the lecturers at the time, they will go back home, get caught up in the usual demands, and life will go on as before.

**An exercise for working in different size groups**

Many people new to group work think that working in different size groups just slows up the process, when there is an urgent need "to get the job done". However, research has shown that both the level of satisfaction after meetings and later commitment to carrying out the decisions made are directly related to (a) how much people feel they had a chance to participate and (b) how much others have responded to their ideas.

The following exercise is to help people experience how different size groups affect the motivation and satisfaction of group members.

**Time**      About 3 hours.

**Materials** Evaluation forms: 3 times the number of participants in the group.

**Preparation before** the exercise.

- Three interesting and equally involving topics need to be chosen by the planning group, and each one put on newsprint.
- Three people need to be asked if they would be willing to act as chairperson, one for each session. These 3 people should have about the same amount of experience with groups.

## Procedure

**Session 1.** Before this session you have asked someone to be chairperson. As animator, you give the whole group the topic for discussion. They are to discuss the topic **in the whole group for 30 minutes.** Animators are observers. (An interesting topic could be, "What are the three most important things the government (or church) could do to solve the problems of youth today?")

**Evaluation**   When the session is finished after 30 minutes, the animator asks each person, individually, to answer the following questions. When they are completed, collect the forms.

---

**Evaluation Form**

1. How involved were you in this discussion? Indicate the degree of your involvement by ticking one of the following:
   a. very involved
   b. involved
   c. not involved
   d. bored
2. How happy were you about the decisions being made? Tick only one below:
   a. very happy
   b. happy
   c. not happy
   d. very disappointed
3. What helped and what hindered our group from working well together?

---

**Session 2.**   In this session, the animator introduces the new chairperson and then introduces the new topic for discussion, which is put up on the wall on newsprint. The animator also states that this time the groups will discuss the topic first in **groups of 6s** for 20 minutes. The last 10 minutes they will share in the whole group, and the new chairperson will facilitate at that point. The animator puts the people into groups of 6s. The animator stops the discussion after the total 30 minutes.

**Evaluation**   New evaluation forms are given to people to fill out. They are collected and kept separate from the ones given in the first session.
>   (Note. A possible topic for session 2 could be, "What are the main obstacles to women being leaders in church/national affairs, and what three things can we do to involve them?")

**Session 3.** In this last session, the animator introduces the new chairperson and then introduces the new topic for discussion, which is put up for all to see. (Possible topic: "What is the rightful role of Parish/District Councils? Name 3 areas they could be responsible for.") The animator also states that this time the group will share first in **groups of 3s** for 10 to 15 minutes and then with the whole group for the last 15 minutes. The animator puts the people into groups of 3s, and after 10 to 15 minutes brings them back to the whole group. The chairperson now leads the group until the 30 minutes have finished.

**Evaluation**   New evaluation forms are given to people. They are collected and kept separate from the others.

**Break**   This is a good time for a tea break. During this break, the animators record the answers to questions 1 and 2 on newsprint indicating how people rated their involvement and satisfaction.

**Final discussion**

The animator shares the results from questions 1 and 2 with the whole group. The group is asked to go into groups of 4s (for a change) and discuss the following questions:

1.   As animators or group facilitators, what do we think about some people being bored or not happy with decisions made?
     Do we think this is usual — thus we need not bother about it? Or is this our responsibility? Why or why not?
     (Note: Most likely only a few people have indicated boredom. Then the question is, are we satisfied even so?)
2.   What have we learnt about methods during this session?
3.   How does this affect our work with people?

**Share insights in the whole group.**

## 3. DIFFERENT GROUPINGS FOR DIFFERENT PURPOSES

In a 4 –5– day workshop of about 30 people, different kinds of groupings are required at different times.

### a. First phase: meeting new people

At the beginning the main need is to create a learning climate and build a community. For introductions, sharing concerns, etc., it is useful to ask people to choose 1 or 2 people they do not yet know to discuss certain questions. This means that they do not stick with those people they knew before the workshops. Everyone begins to know most of the people on a personal basis. This makes a tremendous difference to the spirit of the workshop.

### b. Second phase: interest groups

Once the concerns have been identified people will find most satisfaction if they can go deeply into the questions they are most concerned about. Of course they like to choose these groups themselves.

The quickest and easiest way to arrange this is to identify the main interests, and write each in large letters on a separate piece of paper. These papers are taped at different places around the room, and everyone is asked to go to the group they are most interested in. Sometimes it does not matter if there are not enough people to discuss one topic suggested. At other times some people can be asked to make a second choice.

The pace of the workshop should change now, and these groups should meet for longer periods of time. Otherwise the discussions will become superficial.

### Groups of similar background

In order to develop better understanding between groups that have different views of problems, needs, etc., it can be helpful to put people into similar groups (e.g. all women together, all youth under 20, all married men, all priests, etc). In these groups they can sometimes discuss more freely, and then share their insights with the whole group more effectively than an isolated individual could do in a mixed group. This is particularly important to enable groups that are usually more silent, to be heard by those who are usually more dominant.

### Continuity groups for daily reflection

It can be helpful to have groups of 4 people who feel at ease with one another and can reflect together on what are the most important things they have learnt so far, how they can apply them at home, any things they are worried about, etc. These groups should not report back to the big group, but can make any suggestions they want to the planning group.

Sometimes this gives people an opportunity to speak in their own language, which can be a great relief after concentrating on a second language most of the time.

The easiest way to form these groups is to ask each person to find a partner with whom they would feel at ease, and then to ask each pair to find another pair.

**c.     Third phase: planning groups**

If the workshop is not to be merely a talkshop, but is to lead to action and change, it is important to leave enough time for planning in the groups that will be *working together in the future.* These can be regional groups, parish groups, members of a particular organisation (e.g. youth club, women's groups, etc.).

> **There is usually far more follow-up if workshops are attended by teams rather than by isolated individuals.**

**Whole group**

Most participants do like to keep a sense of the whole group and of what is going on in other groups, so some sharing should be done in the whole group.

**Long reports from small groups often become boring. It is usually best to take one point at a time from a group,** asking any other group that has dealt with that point to add their contribution immediately afterwards. This ensures that the report back is far more lively and participatory.

Whole groups meetings can be used for demonstrations, short presentations of theory, instructions, simulations and some discussion of issues and summaries. But prolonging discussions on issues in the whole group when the majority begin to get passive or uninterested is not helpful to the movement of the group.

---

**Discussion questions**

1.  Is it possible to use different groupings even in formal meetings? Why or why not? How?
2.  How could the use of different groupings help the groups you work with become more effective?

---

**4.     TIMING AND PACING**

One of the most important responsibilities of an animator is to make the most of the energy in the group. Good timing and pace is an essential part of this. (S)he needs to be very sensitive and watch for non-verbal cues to judge whether people are ready for a change of group. Often in a big group, a few are still very interested when the majority have become bored or sleepy. The animator needs to check whether participants are getting a "glazed stare" in their eyes, looking at their watches, out of the window, or at the ceiling. All these are signs it would be good to get into small buzz groups or take a short break. Sometimes those who are still deeply involved in a discussion can continue, while the others do something else.

The animator must constantly make judgments about when a discussion has gone on long enough, or when the time planned should be extended because people are very much involved in something that is important to them.

> People remain far more interested and involved if there is variety of activity and a good balance between:
> - work in small groups and big groups,
> - some time for talking and some for listening,
> - being active and also thoughtful, and
> - working quickly and then slower.

## 5. BRAINSTORMING

This is a technique to gather as many ideas as possible, before deciding which ones to discuss in depth. It avoids the frequent mistake of spending too much time discussing the first suggestion offered so that not enough time is left to discuss other, and perhaps better, suggestions.

It is necessary to give people a little time in 2s or 3s to bring their ideas to the top of their minds first. The brainstorming should then be done quickly, one animator drawing one point at a time from participants and another recording on newsprint. Comments and discussion on individual points should not be allowed until all the suggestions have been collected.

Brainstorming is only a starting technique. Afterwards, in-depth discussion of individual points is necessary, otherwise the group will feel that everything is dealt with superficially.

## 6. USE OF NEWSPRINT

Recording on newsprint is another skill and is not as easy as it looks.

It is most helpful
- during brainstorming when one needs a list of the main concerns,
- agenda for a meeting,
- main insights from an exercise (e.g. difficulties in listening, etc.). When people see their suggestions written down (and later included in the program by the planning group) they get a sense that their contributions are taken seriously and this fosters a spirit of trust.

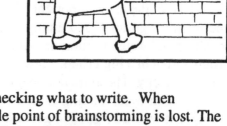

As the writer has her or his back to the group most of the time, one needs two people, one to draw the ideas out of the group, and one to write. When using newsprint one should:
- try to summarise each contribution in a few words,
- use, where possible, the key words of the participants so that they recognise their own contributions,
- avoid slowing up the process, by constantly checking what to write. When people in the group start dictating to the writer, the whole point of brainstorming is lost. The whole process can be slowed up to the point where people lose interest.

A visual record is important to keep ideas and goals clear. **But too much newsprint can be a distraction.** Sometimes it is best to limit what will be written (e.g. only practical suggestions for action – not every point discussed by a group). It is never necessary to write what people saw happening in a code.

When an exchange of ideas in depth is taking place, with participants trying out new thoughts and building on one another's ideas, writing on newsprint can be an annoying distraction and should be abandoned. A person can then write notes in a notebook for later use.

The main purpose of newsprint is to keep a record that the group, or the planning group, can use later. Things that do not need to be kept can be written on a blackboard, e.g. headings of a short theory if a handout is to be given later.

Every writer should check to see that his or her writing on newsprint can be read easily from the opposite side of the room.

---

### THE NEED FOR GROUP SOLIDARITY

"Culture and tradition, women said, could be chains that bind people. "Our traditions and culture make us believe that we are weak and inferior. Even our churches make us believe that we are weak. So our traditions and our culture discriminate against us . . .

"We need women's organisations because of the special problems that we face as women. In our separate women's groups we can talk about all these things. Because women are not taught to be in competition with each other, we can talk easily to each other. We can look at how women see themselves, why we think we are weak, and we can learn to have confidence in ourselves and our abilities.

"In our groups we can share our problems. **A problem shared is a problem cut in half.** When we come together to discuss our problems we also learn that talk is not just gossip but leads to action. In our groups we can educate ourselves about the struggle in our country. This we can use to teach our children."

*Vukani Makhosikazi:*
*South African Women Speak*
p. 265

---

### CONSIDERATION FOR PEOPLE

"Running right through our development activities must be this kind of consideration for people. No one who ignores the feelings of people can be a socialist, for socialism is about people. And it is not good enough just to think of the 'masses', and how they will benefit from a particular project in the long run. The masses are the people considered together: if you do not care about a small group of people then it is at least open to doubt whether you really care about the large group."

— Julius Nyerere
*Freedom and Development*, p. 104.

# D. Introduction exercises

Most of us are a little unsure of ourselves, especially in a group of strangers. People need help in a new group to get to know the others quickly so that they are no longer strangers. Left to themselves, most people will stick to the group they already know, so free time, unstructured social evenings, etc., at the beginning of a workshop do not help new people much to get to know one another.

Introductions, with a definite structure, are more helpful and the following suggested exercises can be a step to start building trust.

People often need both (a) an overview of the group as a whole, i.e. an opportunity to see what kind of people are attending the workshop and (b) an opportunity to start getting to know new people on a more personal level.

## 1. GESTURE WITH YOUR NAME

This is an excellent exercise to start off a workshop. It gives every participant an opportunity to say the name by which they would like to be called during the workshop, and all the other participants an opportunity to repeat the name twice. It also invites each person to say something about themselves non-verbally in a way that is not threatening for shy people but gives those who want it an opportunity to be creative. It also provokes lots of laughter which helps to break the ice. By offering their names and their gesture, each person symbolically takes out their "membership ticket" in the group. The group recognises their presence and welcomes each one personally.

**Procedure**

a. Ask people to sit or stand in a circle in which they can all see each other's faces, and where they have a bit of room to stretch.

b. Explain that each person in the circle will be asked to say loudly and clearly enough for all to hear, "I am —", and give the name by which she would like to be called. At the same time she is asked to do a gesture which expresses something about who she is, or how she is feeling at the moment. This may be reaching out her arms to all in the group, hiding her face, skipping across the floor, or anything else that occurs to her, the more spontaneous the better.

c. The group responds by all saying together, "This is —", repeating her name, and at the same time repeating the gesture, enlarging it a little as they do so. They then add "Welcome, —" and repeat her name again.

d. The facilitator begins by introducing herself in this way and doing a gesture, choosing one that stimulates people's imagination, but is not so elaborate that others feel intimidated or competitive.

e. The group responds as described above.

f. One of the people beside the facilitator is then asked to introduce herself in this way and the process continues right around the circle until everyone has had a turn.

**Time**  Less than one minute per person.

**Materials**  None.

## 2. STAND UP IF ... this applies to you

A new group of people is usually curious to know something about the background and experience of others who are participating in the workshop. An easy way to do this quickly, especially in a large group, is to prepare a list of questions relating to relevant types of experience which other participants might like to know about. The facilitator asks all those to whom each question applies, to stand up for a few moments, so that others can see who they are. The participants soon get a sense of the rich variety of experience present among the members of the workshop. This encourages them to see one another, as well as the staff, as resource people.

The list needs to be tailor-made for each different group and it is important to ensure that everybody will have the opportunity to stand up a number of times. Those preparing the list need to be very sensitive to the feelings of participants, and to make sure that they do not hurt or embarrass anybody, especially in the introductory phase of a workshop. The aim is to help the whole group recognise the relevance of many different types of experience. If there is a certain level of trust, one can introduce certain questions which would be inappropriate in another setting. For instance, in a workshop dealing with unemployment one might ask people to stand up if they have ever experienced unemployment themselves. Then this experience, painful though it may have been at the time, can be seen as an asset, enabling one to understand more deeply the people the group hopes to help, rather than as something to be ashamed of.

Skills which may contribute to the life of the group can be highlighted, with questions around music, drawing, acting, dancing, organising games, preparing rituals, etc. One can suggest that people watch carefully who stands up, in order to spot people they would like to meet with, either formally or informally, in between sessions.

It is best if two different facilitators alternate in asking the different questions, as the change of voices adds more vitality to the process. It is also important to intersperse some questions which will raise a laugh to lighten the atmosphere in the group, e.g. "Stand up if you are afraid of spiders ..."

### Procedure

a. Introduce the exercise as a way of building trust in the group (see above).

b. Ask the participants to stand if the statement applies to them, giving them enough time to see the others who are standing.

c. A sample list might begin with the following questions:

**"Stand up if ...**
- you were born within 50 miles of this place
- in another province ... name each one ...
- in another country ... name them

- you grew up on a farm
- in a small town
- in a big city

- your home language is Xhosa ... Sotho ... Kikuyu ... Spanish ... English
- you speak a second ... third ... fourth ... fifth language
- you have ever been a teacher ... social worker. . . farmer ... nurse, etc.
- planted a vegetable garden ... had a dog ... gone fishing ...

19

Other questions may be prepared around family situation, occupation, class experience, movements or groups one may have belonged to, favourite recreation activities and hobbies, books read or films seen, fears and worries, functions within an organisation and so on.

**Time**       10 – 15 minutes

**Materials**   List of topics


## 3.    BRAINSTORMING AND INTERVIEWS

This exercise helps people think about "what" they need to know about others in order to work with them. It also helps in giving each person a chance to speak in a large group. Often shy people think they cannot speak, but this opportunity helps to set a climate that everyone's contribution is needed and valued.


**Procedure**

a.   Ask the people to discuss with someone next to them, *"What would we like to know about the people here in order to work well with them?"* Be sure to be clear that they are not now interviewing the person they are talking to, but preparing to make a list of things that they think are important to know about all the other people in the room.

b.   Give them about 5 minutes to discuss this.

c.   Brainstorm, getting one point at a time from people, writing up points on newsprint.

d.   When this is finished, ask people to find a partner, someone they do **not** know. They are then to interview the partner (without taking notes). Build in the listening exercise at this point if you wish.

> Person A interviews B  (5 minutes)
> A checks what (s)he heard from B  (2 minutes)
> Person B interviews A  (5 minutes)
> B checks what (s)he heard from A  (2 minutes)

e.   If there are fewer than 35 people in the group, then all can come back to the whole group. Each person is given two minutes to introduce her/his partner to the whole group. If it is a large group, you can put them into groups of 8 (4 pairs) to introduce their partner to others.

f.   To keep the introductions brief in the whole group, a time limit of 1 minute each can be given.


**Time**       Depends on the size of the whole group, but with 30 – 40 people, this takes 2 hours.

**Materials**   Newsprint, tape, felt pens (blackboard).

## 4.  DRAWINGS

Some people are shy to express themselves in words. This exercise gives a person a chance to reflect on "who am I?" before sharing it in the group.

**Procedure**
a.  Ask people to form groups of 5 or 6, finding people they do **not** know.
b.  Give each participant about 10 –15 minutes to *"draw a symbol of some experience in their past life which has had an important influence on the type of person they have become today"*. (People are often hesitant to draw at first as they feel they are not good artists, but if you can make them realise this is not an art competition, it often leads to very good sharing.)
c.  When they have finished, each person introduces her/himself to the others in the small group of 6. Animators should enter into these introductions; however, one person should remain outside a group to help ensure the groups come back at the right time.
d.  If the whole group is not larger than 40 people, you can then instruct each person to take responsibility for introducing one other person from their small group to the whole group (e.g. A introduces B, B introduces C, C introduces D, etc.). When they come to the large group, each person has 1 minute to introduce that person to the whole group.

**Time**  Depends on the size of the whole group, but with 30 – 40 people this takes about  1 – 1¹/2 hours.

**Materials**  Paper and crayons.


## 5.  THE PIE

This exercise gives people a chance to think about themselves before sharing with a group. It can help people to share more deeply than with brief introductions.

**Procedure**
a.  Give each person a piece of paper and  pencil if necessary.
b.  Form groups of 6s of people who do **not** know each other well. Ask each person to take 5 – 10 minutes  to draw a pie and divide it into slices representing various parts of their lives: for example, a certain part of their life concerns family,  work, recreation, outside work, interests, social activities, etc. The animator should demonstrate the dividing of the pie on newsprint before having each person  drawing his/her own.
c.  Use the same procedures for sharing, as in the drawing exercise.

**Time**  About 1 – 1¹/2 hours.

**Materials**  Blackboard (to demonstrate first), paper, pencils.

## 6.   THE JOURNEY OF MY LIFE*

Some groups know each other from work or from other meetings, but may not have shared with each other much about themselves. This exercise is very good to help people move into sharing more deeply with each other. It is not good to start with it when the members of the group does not know each other at all. It is not used in whole group sharing.

### Procedure
a.   Ask participants to draw on a piece of paper their life line illustrating their life, showing the ups and downs, particularly significant periods and events and

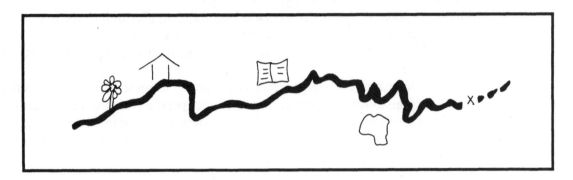

people, how they felt about them, etc. Mark X at the present point and continue the line into the future. One might ask the people to include a symbol for each significant period. Assure the group that no one should feel pressured to share anything they do not wish to share in the group. We all have the right to keep certain aspects of our lives private. And yet the more we are able to share, the more we help to build a foundation of trust in the group.

b.   This life line should then be shared in groups of 4 or 5 people **only.**
(Note: This is not a useful exercise for helping a whole group to get to know everyone. It involves sharing deeply and it is not something that can be rushed. However, knowing a small group well at some points contributes more to trust, than knowing a little bit about a lot of people.)

**Time**       45 minutes to 1 hour.

**Materials**  Paper, pencils and crayons.

---

* Adapted and developed by David and Jean Poynton.

## 7. PHOTOLANGUAGE*

This exercise either can be used as a means to help people first introduce themselves, or it can be used later to share more deeply with others our concerns, how we see certain questions, etc.

### Procedure

a.  A series of big photographs (at least twice as many as the participants) are spread on tables in a room. We have often found putting them in a nearby room gives more space to the participants to move into groups after they choose a photo.

b.  These photos need to be selected carefully so that
    i.   the participants can identify with the particular photos,
    ii.  they are relevant to the particular theme, and
    iii. they are large and clear.

c.  After participants have formed groups of 4 – 6 people, they are asked to walk around in silence looking at the pictures and "in their minds" to select one or two which would say something about themselves, their values or concerns; something they would be willing to share with the group. This takes 3 – 5 minutes.
    If the group is ready to go more deeply and share more of themselves, the question asked could be, *"Choose a picture which represents an important question for you, or a worry (something which you think about late at night, when you are alone)."* The way you word this question depends on how personally the group wish to share.

d.  After selecting a photo, people are asked to return to their groups. Each one shows the photo he/she chose and explains why he/she chose it.

e.  People can ask questions, but it should be stressed that there are not right or wrong interpretations of a picture. The point is for the group to try to understand what the picture meant to the person who chose it, and only later, if there is time, should others share what it means to them.

**Time**          If in groups of 4 – 6 people, about 45 minutes.

**Materials**     At least twice as many photos as participants.

---

* Adapted from Pierre Babin, *Photo Language,* Lyons, France.

## 8. INTRODUCTIONS ON THE MOVE* (For a large group)

If the group you are to work with is very large, it is very difficult for everyone to know everyone. It is possible to use one of the above exercises in small groups of 6 and then move to the large group with this exercise. This can help the group to get an overview of what the whole group is like.

### Procedure

a. If you have done an introduction in small groups using the "Journey of My Life", The Pie, or Drawing, you then ask each person to pin the paper they have used onto their chest.
Ask all participants to walk around the room and find people they do not know and introduce themselves, sharing what they have drawn or written.

b. If you have not had time to let them share in smaller groups, one can ask each person to write in large writing or draw, on a sheet of paper, 4 – 6 important things about themselves, for example:

  i.   their work
  ii.  their place of living,
  iii. something they have done recently which they are pleased about.

c. When participants have finished writing these things, ask them all to pin these papers on their chests, and walk around the room, introducing themselves and asking questions of others, getting to know one another.

**Time**      About half an hour.

**Materials**  Paper and pins. Pens or felt pens. These are needed for all participants.

---

* Adapted from *A Handbook of Structured Experience for Human Relations Training,* by J. Wm. Pfeiffer and John E. Jones, Vol. III, University Association, San Diego, 1974, p. 3.

## 9.   GROUP INTRODUCTIONS

This method helps members of a small group to get to know each other and the whole group to know something brief about each person. It tends to become more formal and does less to "warm up" the participants. It gives an overview of who are the members of the group and where they are from.

**Procedure 1**

   a.   Ask particular groups of people to meet together (regional teams or members of particular organisations) and get to know each person in the group. One person is selected in the group to be the spokesperson.

   b.   After the small groups have had time to share information about each person, the whole group is called together and the spokesperson introduces each person in the small group to the whole group.

**Time**       Time for this method of introduction depends on how many different groups are represented. Usually it takes 45 minutes to 1 hour.

**Materials**  No materials are necessary.

**Procedure 2**   Group symbols to build a deeper trust

   a.   People are put into groups of 5. They are asked to discuss the backgrounds of each person and try to get to know each other as well as possible.

   b.   After this discussion, the task of each group of 5 is to make a play, a song, a dance, or a drawing which reflects the reality of their group.

   c.   When this is completed, each group presents its play (song, dance, etc.) to the whole group.

**Time**       This exercise takes about 1 hour if there are about 30 participants.

**Materials**  Paper, newsprint, crayons, magazines.

## 10. MOST IMPORTANT EVENTS IN THE LAST SIX MONTHS

When the same group comes back together many times, it is important to build again the spirit of community, getting in touch with what is important for each person at that moment. Although the work of the group is important, the building of personal relationships and deeper communion is equally important. The following exercise is useful for this.

**Procedure**
    a.    Ask each person to take 5 minutes in silence to think about the event which has been most exciting or most discouraging for them personally in the last six months (or since you last met).
    b.    Ask each person to share briefly in the whole group.

**Time**    This exercise is good for a group of not more than 30 people. It takes a few minutes for each person, so expect about 1– 2 hours.

---

### Dialogue and love

Dialogue is not possible without a profound love for the world and for people. Love is both the foundation of dialogue and dialogue itself. Only responsible people — the subjects of their own history — can participate in dialogue, and it cannot exist in a situation of domination.

Domination is like a mental illness of love. Love is an act of courage, not of fear. Love is commitment to other people. No matter where the oppressed are found, the act of love involves commitment to their cause, the cause of liberation. And this commitment, because it is loving, must take place in the form of dialogue. Love is brave and free, it cannot be sentimental or manipulative. If it does not lead to other acts of freedom it cannot really be love. It is only by abolishing a situation of oppression that it is possible to restore love in that situation. If I do not love the world – love life – love people, I cannot enter into dialogue.

### Dialogue cannot exist without humility

How can I enter into a dialogue if I always imagine that others are ignorant, and never become conscious of my own ignorance? How can I enter into dialogue if I see myself as a person apart from others – if I see them only as "its" not as another "I"? How can I enter into dialogue if I consider myself a member of an "in group", the owners of truth and knowledge, the "pure people"?

If I am closed to, and even offended by, the contribution of others; if I fear being displaced, how can I hold a dialogue?

At the point of encounter there are neither utterly ignorant people, nor perfectly wise people. There are only those who attempt together to learn more than they now know.

— Adapted from **Paulo Freire**
CCPD Documents, World Council of Churches,
Geneva, Switzerland, May 1975.

# E. Listening exercises

The most important first step in any process of empowerment is giving those who have been marginalised, alienated or oppressed a new confidence that their experience, their ideas and opinions are valuable and worth listening to. Listening is therefore one of the most important skills for every group member, and especially every animator, to develop.

Most of us are so busy thinking about our own ideas and points of view that we do not listen very attentively to others, unless we think they are experts. For a spirit of trust and appreciation of one another to grow in a group, it is essential that people **listen to one another.** Several listening exercises are suggested and can be helpful. The concentration and attention with which the animator listens to each speaker is the most important factor in developing an attitude of listening in the whole group.

> **A group never becomes a community unless it develops the habit of deep, respectful listening to one another.**

## 1. DIALOGUE OR MONOLOGUE*

This code is useful early in a workshop. It establishes the value of listening; the need for quiet people to speak up; and the need for dominant people to be sensitive to others. The play needs to be practised once before it is used.

**Procedure**

a.  Invite 6 people to prepare a short play in 3 scenes. It is usually better to have all women or all men acting as this avoids people saying, "men always do this ..." or "women always do that ..."

**Scene 1:** Two people meet. One of them starts to talk and gets so excited and involved in what (s)he is saying that (s)he pays no attention to the other. The other tries several times to speak, to ask a question, respond, or make a suggestion, but the first person talks on, so the second person remains silent and gives up trying. (The pair should decide on a topic beforehand.)

---

*   This exercise developed by Fr. John Mutiso and the planning group for a National Development Workshop, Limuru, Kenya, January 1974.

**Scene 2:** Two people meet and both start telling the other what they are concerned about. They each have a different topic. Neither is listening to the other, and both are talking at the same time.

**Scene 3:** Two people meet, greet each other, and start a real dialogue. Each one asks questions about the other's interests, listens and responds to the other's answers, and shares his/her own news and opinions. (A common topic should be decided on beforehand).

b.  One of the animators should stop each play when the point has been made. Usually the first two plays take 1 or 2 minutes and the third play takes a little longer.

c.  The group is divided into 3s to answer the following **questions:**
    i.  What did you see happening in Scene 1?
        What did you see happening in Scene 2?
        What did you see happening in Scene 3?
    ii.  Do these things happen in real life? How?
    iii.  What can we do to help make communication as good as possible in this group?

d.  The whole group come together and shares briefly their answers to the first two questions, and then the animator asks someone to write on newsprint the answers to question 3 only.

e.  The animator summarises the points on question 3 at the end. Keep the newsprint on the wall to provide the group's own "Guidelines for Good Communication".

**Time**     About 45 minutes.

**Materials**  Newsprint, tape, felt pens (or blackboard).

> **He who talks incessantly talks nonsense**
> – Ivory Coast

28

## 2.   LISTENING IN SILENCE

The skill of listening with full attention and "entering into" another person's understanding of himself or herself is the key to good leadership. All of us have difficulties in listening. This exercise helps people understand their own problems of listening.

**Procedure**

a.   The animator introduces the aim of this exercise and explains what the procedure will be.

b.   Groups of 4 – 8 people are best for this exercise.

c.   Each person is asked to talk for 2 or 3 minutes on some subject on which the group is likely to have strong feelings, e.g. "What are some of your experiences and feelings when you are asked to take a leadership role in a group?"
or, "When did you first realise that some people are more privileged than others,
  i.   that others had more privileges than you, **or**
  ii.   that you had more privileges than others."
or, "Describe an event or experience that made you extremely joyful or extremely angry."

d.   The rest of the group (of 4 – 8 people) listen in silence to each person without asking questions or commenting.

e.   Afterwards the animator asks the group:
*"What helped you to listen well and what made it more difficult to listen (or what hindered you from listening well)?"* This can be discussed in groups of 3s.

f.   The whole group comes together, and the answers are listed on two separate sheets of newsprint.

g.   Then the participants are all asked to decide for themselves and write down what they want to work on during the workshop:

   1.   to listen more attentively to others,
   2.   to help others listen to him/her when he/she is speaking.

**Time**      About 1 to 1½ hours.

**Materials**  Newsprint, tape, and felt- tip pens.

> "Women are not thinking of courage
> in relation to the power that means exercising
> might over people . . .
> Rather, it is the power of listening, of patience . . .
> This is a new vision of the power that we,
> as women, have together."
>
> — Nita  Barrow
> A President of the World Council of Churches
> Health Educator, Barbados, West Indies

## 3.  LISTENING PAIRS

It is common that when we disagree with someone, we have the most difficulty listening to them. This exercise is to help develop the skill of listening (even when we disagree) and provides a way of finding out if we truly are listening to others. The exercise should be used once members of a group know each other fairly well.

**Procedure**

a.  Each person is asked to find a partner with whom they know they disagree on a specific subject. They are then asked to discuss this subject, but after each one has spoken, the other must **summarise to the speaker's satisfaction** what has just been said, before they give their own response or point of view.
Note: In this exercise each pair choose for themselves the topic they will discuss.

**Or**

b.  Each person is asked to choose a partner and the animator gives a controversial topic for them to discuss. Again, after each one has spoken the other must summarise to the speaker's satisfaction what has just been said. Only then may (s)he give her or his own response or point of view on the subject.
(Possible topics are: abortion, divorce, women's liberation, socialism/capitalism, etc.)

c.  After either exercise **a** or **b,** the animator should ask the group what difficulties they experienced in listening and list these on newsprint.

d.  Then ask what they can do to improve communication in the group.
Write answers on newsprint.

**Time**      About 1 hour.

**Materials**   Newsprint, tape, felt tip pens.

---

**We need to hear one another into speech.**
— Nelle Morton

---

## 4.　INPUT ON LISTENING TECHNIQUES*

The following input on barriers in listening can be given to a group after any of the above exercises.

### The nature of listening

Listening is an art, a skill, and a discipline. As in the case of other skills, it needs self-control. The individual needs to understand what is involved in listening and develop the necessary self-control to be silent and listen, keeping down his or her own needs and concentrating attention on the other with a spirit of humility.

Listening obviously is based on hearing and understanding what others say to us. **Hearing becomes listening only when we pay attention** to what is said and follow it very closely.

### Barriers and roadblocks in listening

Here is a list of poor listening habits.

### 1.　On-off listening

This unfortunate habit in listening arises from the fact that most people think about 4 times as fast as they can speak. Thus, the listener has 3/4 of a minute of "spare thinking time" in each listening minute. Sometimes s/he uses this extra time to think about his or her own personal affairs, concerns and troubles instead of listening, relating and summarising what the speaker has to say. One can overcome this by paying attention to more than the words, watching non-verbal signs like gestures, hesitation, etc., to pick up the feeling level.

### 2.　Red flag listening – words that cause an emotional reaction.

To some people, certain words cause an emotional reaction (like a red flag to a bull). When we hear them, we get upset and stop listening. These terms vary in every group, society and organisation. The terms "capitalist", "communist", "money", "feminist", "modern youth", "tribalistic", etc., are signals to which some people respond almost automatically. When this signal comes in, we tune out the speaker. We lose contact with her or him, and fail to develop an understanding of that person. The first step in overcoming this barrier is to find out which words start an emotional reaction in us personally, and try to listen attentively and sympathetically, even when they are mentioned.

---

\* Adapted from the Christian Education Leadership Training Program, South Africa.

### 3. Open ears – close mind listening

Sometimes we decide rather quickly that either the subject or the speaker is boring,

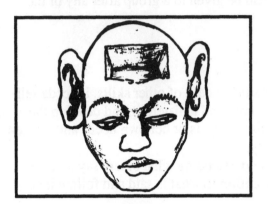

and what is said makes no sense. Often we jump to conclusions that we can predict what (s)he knows or what (s)he will say; thus we conclude, there is no reason to listen because we will hear nothing new if we do. It is much better to listen and find out for sure whether this is true or not.

### 4. Glassy-eyed listening

Sometimes we look at a person intently, and we **seem** to be listening although our

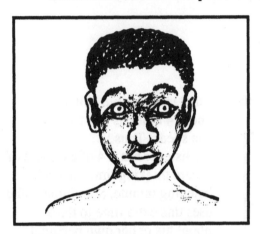

minds may be on other things or in far-distant places. We drop back into the comfort of our thoughts. We get glassy-eyed and often a dreamy expression appears on our faces. We can tell when people look this way. Similarly they can see the same in us, and we are not fooling anyone. Postpone day-dreaming for other times. If you notice many people looking glassy-eyed, find an appropriate moment to suggest a break or a change in pace.

### 5. Too-deep-for-me listening

When we are listening to ideas that are too complex and complicated, we need to force ourselves to follow the discussion and make a real effort to understand it. We may find the subject and speaker quite interesting if we listen and understand what the person is saying. Often if we do not understand, others do not either, and it can help the group to ask for clarification or an example when possible.

### 6. Don't-rock-the-boat listening

People do not like to have their favourite ideas, prejudices, and points of view

overturned: many do not like to have their opinions and judgments challenged. So, when a speaker says something that clashes with what we think or believe, we may unconsciously stop listening or even become defensive and plan a counterattack. Even if we want to do this, it is better to listen; find out what the speaker thinks; get the other side of the question so we can do a better job of understanding and responding constructively.

### Discussion questions

1. When have I had some of these barriers in listening?
2. Where have I seen them happen in groups?

## THREE SHORT INPUTS ON LISTENING

Sometimes, before giving the input, it is useful to ask the group to discuss the following questions in 3s and then share in the whole group.

1. What are our objectives in listening?
2. Can you suggest some "do's and don'ts" of listening?
3. What responses can one give to encourage
   - further talking
   - restatement
   - deeper reflection
   - summarising
   - decision-making?

The following inputs can be given on listening techniques.

### Objectives in listening in any helping relationship

The objectives when we listen to people are both basic and simple.
1. We want people to talk freely and frankly.
2. We want them to cover matters and problems that are important to them.
3. We want them to furnish as much information as they can.
4. We want them to get greater insight and understanding of their problem as they talk it out.
5. We want them to try to see the causes and reasons for their problems and to figure out what can be done about them.

### Some do's and don'ts of listening

In listening we should try to **do** the following:
a. Show interest.
b. Be understanding of the other person.
c. Express empathy.
d. Single out the problem if there is one.
e. Listen for causes of the problem.
f. Help the speaker associate the problem with the cause.
g. Encourage the speaker to develop competence and motivation to solve his or her own problems.
h. Cultivate the ability to be silent when silence is needed.

In listening, **do not** do the following:
a. Argue.
b. Interrupt.
c. Pass judgment too quickly or in advance.
d. Give advice unless it is requested by the other.
e. Jump to conclusions.
f. Let the speaker's emotions react too directly on your own.

33

# LISTENING TECHNIQUES

| Types | Purpose | Possible Responses |
|---|---|---|
| 1. *Clarifying* | 1. To get at additional facts.<br>2. To help the person explore all sides of a problem. | 1. "Can you clarify this?"<br>2. "Do you mean this?"<br>3. "Is this the problem as you see it now?" |
| 2. *Restatement* | 1. To check our meaning and interpretation with the other.<br>2. To show you are listening and that you understand what the other has said. | 1. "As I understand it, your plan is . . ."<br>2. "Is this what you have decided to do . . . and the reasons are . . ." |
| 3. *Neutral* | 1. To convey that you are interested and listening.<br>2. To encourage the person to continue talking. | 1. "I see."<br>2. "I understand."<br>3. "That is a good point." |
| 4. *Reflective* | 1. To show that you understand how the other feels about what (s)he is saying.<br>2. To help the person to evaluate and temper his or her own feelings as expressed by someone else. | 1. "You feel that . . ."<br>2. "It was shocking as you saw it."<br>3. "You felt you didn't get a fair hearing." |
| 5. *Summarising* | 1. To bring all the discussion into focus in terms of a summary.<br>2. To serve as a springboard to discussion of new aspects of the problem. | 1. "These are the key ideas you have expressed . . ."<br>2. "If I understand how you feel about the situation . . ." |

## Listening

"The important role of dialogue
continues through
the whole of a person's life.
    We come to be who we are
through conversation with others.

    This is true on the level of information
and it is also true on the deeper level
of self-knowledge and values of life.

    We listen to others in the family,
the school, the community,
our friends, and our adversaries,
and our consciousness continues to be created
by our response to the reality addressing us.
    We are created
through ongoing communication with others."

## Responding

"The word 'dialogue'
suggests that we are never simply
the creation of the community to which we belong.
    We listen and respond.
    We become ourselves, distinct from others by responding.
These responses are truly our own.
    To the extent that we make them freely
we are responsible
for who we are
and who we come to be as a person.
    Our thinking,
our religion,
our entire mental world
is thus created by a process
in which the entire community is involved,
and yet in which we ourselves
consciously or unconsciously
make the important decisions."

Gregory Baum, *Man Becoming*,
Herder and Herder, N.Y., 1971, pp. 41 – 2

# F.   Trust-building exercises

**Sharing our history.** We have all become who we now are by the experiences and events that make up our history. By sharing significant parts of our history with others, we can lay the foundation of trust. We include a variety of different ways in which this can be done.

## 1.   PAST – PRESENT – FUTURE

This exercise helps people to understand the experiences and situation of others in the past, their present concerns and other hopes for the future. For people under 30, it is best to choose a date 5 years after the present year, and for those a bit older, 10 years before and after the current year.

**Procedure**

a.   This exercise should take place in a group of 4 – 8 people, no more.

b.   In these groups each person shares:
- "Where was I and what was important to me 5 (or 10) years ago?"
  After each one has shared the above, then each one shares:
- "Where do I feel I am now and what is important to me this year?"
  Then each shares:
- "Where would I like to be, what would I like to be doing and what changes would I like to see in my life in 5 (or 10) years' time?"

**Time**   This exercise is best as an evening activity, so groups can go on as long as they wish.

**Materials**   None needed. Questions could be written ahead of time on newsprint or on a blackboard.

## 2.   7 – 12 YEARS OLD

The aim of this exercise is to build trust through sharing some of our childhood experiences. We choose age 7 – 12 because this is a period of our lives that was "given" to us, not made by us, and we can remember it well enough to reflect upon it. Also at that age there is a certain equality. We get away from the barriers created by prestige and position.

It helps, in a mixed group, to understand differences of culture and common human experiences.

**Procedure**

    a.    Groups of 4 – 6 people, not more.

    b.    Each one shares their answers to number 1, then each shares number 2, etc.

          1.    Where was I and what was important to me during the time I was 7 – 12 years old?

          2.    Who was the most important person (influence) in my life at that time?

          3.    When was the first time God became more than a word for me?

          4.    Choose one experience, or event, which had a decisive influence on leading you to make an important decision which has brought you to where you are now.

**Time**        This is best used as an evening activity when groups can end when they finish and do not feel rushed.

**Materials**    Have the questions written up on the board or on newsprint.

## 3.   RIVER OF LIFE

A river is a very meaningful symbol in many cultures, and most people find it quite natural and very stimulating to think of their own lives in terms of a river. Deepak Chopra writes that the river of our life always runs between two banks: one of pain and one of joy. We need both banks as we cannot know the joy without the sorrow. This exercise is very useful as a personal reflection, leading to greater self-knowledge, and also as the basis for a small group sharing, leading to greater trust in the group.

**Procedure**

    a.    Give each person a sheet of plain paper and make plenty of crayons of different colours available.

    b.    Ask each to draw the river of their own life, going right back to the source (the early years in their families), the different periods of their lives, such as quiet peaceful times, and wild stormy times (of rapids and waterfalls). Major influences which contributed to the growth of your river can be shown as tributaries and labelled. And small drawings, showing the important people, events, and experiences, can be drawn beside the river.

    c.    Encourage the group to use colours to express different moods at different periods of their lives.

    d.    Give 10 – 15 minutes for the drawing. Then ask people to form groups of 3 – 5 to share the experience illustrated by the river.

    e.    It is not advisable to share in a large group, but if people wish they can put the drawings on the wall and explain them informally to each other.

**Time**        One hour or more.

**Materials**    Paper and crayons for all participants.

## 4. TREE OF LIFE

A tree, like a river, is one of the universal symbols of life. This exercise helps people reflect on their own lives in greater depth.

**Procedure**

a. Ask each person to close their eyes and imagine what kind of tree represents their life as they experience it now. It might be a very strong oak, a weeping willow, a faithful mango tree or a young sapling.

b. Ask each person to draw the tree of their own life.

   i. The roots represent
- the family from which we come,
- strong influences which have shaped us into the person we are now.

   ii. The trunk represents the structure of our life today
- job
- family
- organisations, communities, movements to which we belong.

   iii. The leaves represent our sources of information
- newspapers
- radio, television
- books
- reports
- friends and contacts

   iv. The fruits represent our achievements
- projects we have organised
- programs
- groups we have started or helped to develop
- materials we have produced

   v. The buds represent our hopes for the future. Thorns can represent the difficulties in our life.

c. Give the group about 20 minutes to do this.

d. Share in groups of 3 – 5. If possible, it is good to do this in an open-ended session (e.g. in the evening) when groups can continue to share for as long as they wish.

   **Time**       At least one hour.

   **Materials**   Paper and crayons for all participants.

## 5.    CLASS ORIGIN – CLASS OPTION

This exercise is particularly useful after a discussion on social class, after playing the simulation Star Power, or after explaining the dynamic model (see Book III).

In any group committed to liberation, those involved all need to come to terms with their own class origins. We need to recognise how this has affected our values and reactions. As Amilcar Cabral recognised, real commitment to the poor, the deprived and the oppressed involves a conscious choice (option) from those who come from more privileged backgrounds – and this option involves class "suicide".

We need constantly to check whether we are claiming unfair privileges and to what extent our society is moving towards equality.

> **"Equality is an ideal. We may never reach it, but unless we aim at equality we will find that our society is becoming more and more unequal."**
>
> — Raphael Kaplinsky

### Procedure

a.    Either type or photocopy the table on the next page for each participant, **or** write it on newsprint.

b.    Ask each participant to reflect on their own life and then fill in the table, starting at the top. It should be pointed out that top sections are "given", the child has no choice about these (and therefore there is no cause for guilt). But each step up involves increasing freedom of choice, and we are personally responsible for the next sections.

c.    Give the group 10 – 15 minutes to do this.

d.    Then ask them to share in groups of 3 – 5 people.

e.    In the whole group ask people to share:

   i.    What are some of the major ways in which we are affected by our class background?

   ii.   How can we tell whether we are genuinely making an option in the struggle of the poor, the deprived, and the oppressed, and working effectively in the process of transformation?

Note:    This exercise is important for self-knowledge and trust-building, particularly in a situation where the class conflict is sharp, and where there is much suspicion.

**Time**    One hour or more.

**Materials**    Duplicated copies of the form.

Education:

# CLASS ORIGIN – CLASS OPTION FORM*

| | Description | Effects |
|---|---|---|
| | | How does each of your answers on the left affect your class awareness and political choices now? |

## Class Origin

Family:

Father's work:

Mother's work:

Home neighbourhood:

Education:

Movements affecting you during youth:

## Class Situation

Name of your sources of information:

Media:

Newspapers:

Books:

People you talk to:

Other:

Occupation:

Present neighbourhood:

## Class Option

Describe type of society you want:

*Adapted from the Ecumenical Institute for the Development of Peoples (INODEP), Paris

40

# 6. POTATO EXERCISE*

This exercise is useful early in a workshop to get people to share feelings about themselves and their relationships with others in a non-threatening way and thus build trust. It can also be a lot of fun. It is best to use it in the evening.

## Procedure

a. The group sits in a circle and each person chooses a potato from a basket passed around quickly. The potatoes should be more or less the same size.

b. Ask them to examine their potatoes carefully. Look at your potato, get the feel of it, its weight, its smell, its peculiarities.

Discuss the characteristics of your potato with the person next to you. Be able to recognise it with your eyes shut, for you will will have to find it from among all the other potatoes in this group with eyes shut!

c. In twos, one person shuts eyes, the other holds both potatoes. The one with eyes shut must pick his/her potato. Reverse procedure.

d. Do this in groups of 4s (and if necessary in 8s).

e. Finally the whole group sits in a circle. The potatoes are collected, and then passed from hand to hand behind people's backs. (This has the same purpose as shutting the eyes.) As each person recognises their own potato, they keep it without looking at it. Keep passing the other potatoes around until all are claimed.

f. The game ends when all (or at least the majority) have found their potatoes (i.e. within a reasonable time).

## Discussion questions

1. What was your first impression when you were given your potato?
   What did you do to identify yours?
2. What feelings did you experience during the process?
3. What have I learnt about myself?
4. What have I learnt about relations with others?
5. What are the implications of this exercise for living together in a community?

   **Time**  One hour with discussion

   **Materials**  At least one potato for each participant and a large basket.

---

\* Adapted from the Lemon exercise, introduced by Father Xavier Manjooran, Gujarat India, International DELTA, Phase II, Ahero, Kenya, July 1977.

## 7.   BUILDING UNITY ACROSS AGE, RACE, CLASS AND SEX

The aim of the following two exercises is to help people become aware of the obstacles that exist for people of different backgrounds, especially when we try to work together in mixed groups.

**Procedure 1**      (Skill practice)

a.   The participants are first put into very mixed groups to accomplish a given task. The mixed groups should be of 5 or 6 people, mixing up as thoroughly as possible the different types of people participating.
   The task should be something practical and relevant to as many of them as possible. (E.g. "Plan a program to involve people of all ages in the community in a Health Care Program", **or** "Plan a program to involve all the parishioners in a meaningful way in parish activities during the next six  months.")

b.   Each mixed group should write their proposal on newsprint and explain it  briefly to the whole group.

c.   Redivide the participants into homogeneous\* groupings, e.g. all women,  youth, teachers, catechists, priests, sisters, etc, together.

d.   Ask each homogeneous group to discuss what difficulties they found:
   1.   in communicating in the previous task with people of different back- grounds (age, sex, occupation, tribe, nationality, educational background, etc.)
   2.   in communicating at home with people of different backgrounds. (Write on newsprint.)

e.   At this point it might be wise to spend a few minutes in the whole group brainstorming points which should be remembered in giving and receiving feedback.

f.   In the whole group, each homogeneous group shares what difficulties they experienced and what helped them to overcome these difficulties in the mixed group. The animator's role here is to help the different groups to hear each other without getting defensive.

**Time**      About 2 to 3 hours. It can be used for half a day or even a full day, depending on how deeply you want to go into each task.

**Materials**   Newsprint and felt pens for each group.

---

\* 'Homogeneous' means 'coming from a similar experience or background'.

## Procedure 2    Two fishbowls, then 3s*

Sometimes it is helpful to have many viewpoints expressed on a subject of particular concern to a group. This exercise is a very creative effort to have those most involved speak first, and then to hear others more openly.

a.    One-third of the group in a specific role (e.g. women, party leaders, priests) are asked to form a fishbowl and discuss two questions:
1.   What do you see as your role in society?
2.   What are the obstacles to fulfilling it?

b.    After 15 minutes each person from the first fishbowl withdraws and asks a new person, whose views they would like to hear, to go into a second fishbowl. The second group discusses the same two questions.

c.    After 15 minutes each person from the original fishbowl is asked to form a group of 3 with the person they chose from the second fishbowl, plus a third person who has been in the outer circle, to discuss the similarities and conflicting ideas in the two fishbowls.

d.    The whole group can be brought together to discuss solutions to this problem. This should be a discussion, and newsprint is not necessarily needed.

**Time**        About 1¹⁄₂ to 2 hours.

**Materials**    None.

---

* Introduced by a learning team, Training of Trainers program, Phase II, Sagana, Kenya, 1975.

## The objectives of our struggle

"Who is the enemy and what is his nature? The enemy of Africa is often confused with the white man. Skin colour is still a factor used by many to determine the enemy. There are historical and social reasons and lived facts which consolidate this idea on our continent . . .

"I do not think that the national liberation struggle is directed towards inverting systems of oppression in such a way that the master of today will be the slave of tomorrow. To think in this way is to go against the current of history. Attitudes of social revenge can never be what we want, which is the freedom of people . . .

"What we want is to establish a new society where black and white can live together. Naturally, and so as not to be misinterpreted, I must add that the democratic process must be exercised in such a way that the most exploited masses (who are black) have control of political power, since they can go furthest in establishing proper rights for all.

"A people's struggle for polititical power, for economic independence, for the restoration of cultural life, to end alienation, for relations with all people on a basis of equality and fraternity – these are the objectives of our struggle."

Agostino Neto,
*The African Liberation Reader,*
Zed Press, London, 1982,
pp. 210 – 212

## Mutual Support:  The Basis for Action

"In struggling to come to terms with the pervasiveness of evil in our life together – for example with anti-Semitism, racism, heterosexism, economic exploitation, and their violent interconnections – I have become increasingly interested in probing the character of that which is radically good in our common life: our power in mutual relation as the basis of our creative and liberating possibilities, literally the only basis of our hope for the world.

"And as we nurture our common goodness, are we better able to deal with evil? Are we wiser, more courageous, more patient with ourselves and others in this world as we learn to take seriously our power for touching the Sacred, our power for creating and sustaining right relation? Does this strengthen our desire, commitment, and ability to make no peace with oppression? Does the experience of mutuality  teach us more fully what it means to live serenely – in quiet confidence that, regardless of the toll of violence, betrayal, and evil in our lives, nothing can separate us from the power of good, the power in right relation, which Christians and other theists may choose to name the love of God?"

Rev. Carter Heyward,
*Touching Our Strength,*
p. 18

**Willingness to change**

"From the beginning then,
there are moments
when the word addressed to us
makes us abandon the world
of our own making,
and enter upon new life.

Dialogue is not simply
a giving and receiving of information;
it does not change a person simply
by expanding their knowledge.

Again and again
as we are in dialogue with others
we must hear the painful word
which overcomes us,
and draws forth a response in us,
that transforms life.

The word addressed to us
at those moments
reveals to us the truth
of which we are afraid.

It pierces the screen we have put up
between ourselves and reality.

Then we must either flee from this word
and hide behind defences,
or open ourselves to it,
go through the painful passage
from our shallow understanding
to greater depth,
and receive the truth
that has been spoken to us.

**Conversion**

"Sometimes dialogue
is happy sharing;
but in the course of life
there are those important
and frequent moments
when dialogue means conversion.

Because we have listened,
because we were willing
to let go the little world
we had made for ourselves,
because we gained a new understanding of reality,
we have become persons in a new way.

Our response
to the world addressed to us
helps to make us who we are.

### Self-knowledge and new life

"Sometimes the call addressed to us
has a very special force.

It reveals to us who we are,
it judges us,
it summons us to grow,
it demands a reply.

It leaves us two choices:
either we choose to be deaf,
and thus harden our opposition to life
or we open ourselves to the truth
and to the possibility of new life.

The Christian,
who has met the Word of God
in Scripture,
and experiences life with faith,
recognises this special word,
arising in human conversation,
as God's word,
present in one's own life,
     summoning,
     judging,
     life-giving."

Gregory Baum,
*Man Becoming,* ibid., pp. 43 – 44

# Chapter 6

# Leadership and participation

**This chapter includes:**

A. Leadership ........................................................................ 49
B. Content and process ........................................................ 53
C. Shared leadership ........................................................... 59
   Exercises on participation ............................................. 61
D. Self- and mutual criticism ............................................. 65
   Exercises on feedback .................................................... 68
E. Exercises on cooperation .............................................. 82
F. Group reaction to the animator ................................... 89

47

# Chapter 6
# Leadership and participation

## A. Leadership

Some people regard leadership as a mysterious, "charismatic" quality, which some people have and some people do not have. It can also be seen as a **skill** that many people can develop if they are willing to take time
- observing what goes on in groups,
- identifying clearly the main needs of groups,
- learning ways of dealing with these needs,
- practising these skills in many different situations,
- taking people's feelings seriously,
- listening to feedback about others' reactions to their own behaviour as a leader,
- making changes in their behaviour, so that people will respond in a positive and not a negative way to them.

It takes sensitivity, humility, and love to develop one's skills as a leader, and it takes a number of years of practice.

### Animator/facilitator/coordinator

The style of leadership is extremely important in any program aiming at full participation of the community in a liberating process and self-reliant development. There are many styles of group leadership. Leadership may be authoritarian, consultative or enabling, as we see in the table found in Chapter 10, Book III.

Though authoritarian leadership may be necessary at times of danger or when a group is struggling for survival, such leadership does not foster initiative, creativity or responsibility in the members of the group. Authoritarian leadership tends to make people act as obedient robots, which do not think for themselves. They may accept this situation for a while, but later people with initiative and creativity will start to rebel.

## PARTICIPATION IN LOCAL POLITICS

In an imaginary future society, novelist Marge Piercy describes local participation in decision-making. "There was nothing people liked so much as a good political fight about principles or ecological correctness or the constant nurturing of true equality. [People] could scream at each other. Everybody could take sides, persuade, entreat, scheme, manipulate, all in the name of some higher goal. Eventually some dim consensus would be patted together and the peace of utter fatigue would descend. It was one of the major sports of the free town.

"Here politics was still a participatory rather than a spectator sport. Every last voter expected to voice her or his opinion at some length and to be courted or denounced. The right to stand up and make a speech for the guaranteed three minutes on any point was a birthright of all: the right to bore your neighbours, the right to spout utter nonsense, while all around you openly groaned . . ."

Marge Piercy,
*Body of Glass,*
p. 547

## COLLECTIVE LEADERSHIP

"But to lead collectively is not and cannot be, as some suppose, to give to all and everyone the right of uncontrolled views and initiatives, to create disorders, empty arguments, a passion for meetings without results . . .

"In the framework of collective leadership, we must respect the opinion of more experienced people who for their part must help the others with less experience to learn and to improve their work. Combat the spirit of the 'big man', the traditional chief, boss or foreman among responsible workers . . . Combat the spirit of closed circles, an obsession with secrecy among some persons, personal questions and the ambition to give orders.
Collective leadership must strengthen the leadership capability of [all] and create specific circumstances where full use is made of all members.

"Collective leadership means leadership made by a group of persons and not by one alone or by some persons in the group.
To lead collectively, in a group, is to:
- study questions jointly,
- find their best solutions,
- take decisions jointly,
- benefit from the experience and intelligence of each person.
To lead collectively is to
- [give] the opportunity of thinking and acting,
- demand that people take responsibility within their competence,
- [require that people] take initiative . . .
To lead collectively is to
- coordinate the thought and action of those who form the group,
- derive the greatest return in the accomplishment of the group's tasks, within the limits of their competence and in the framework of the activities and the interests of the organisations."

Amilcar Cabral,
*Unity and Struggle,*
Copyright © 1979 by PAIGC.

Reprinted by permission of *Monthly Review Press,* New York, 1979, pp. 247–248

**The role of a facilitator** is to **provide a process** which will help the group to discuss their own content in the most satisfactory and productive way possible. The facilitator is neutral about the content of the meeting, and does not have much stake in the decisions that are taken. A facilitator is mainly concerned with process, not with content.

The facilitator's responsibility is to ensure that there is good communication in the group and that all the members are satisfied with, and fully committed to, the decisions taken.

In some cases, a facilitator is not from the community. A facilitator who comes from outside a community may challenge the group about the implications and consequences of their plans, but ultimately, the group must "own" their plans, not follow ideas from outside.

**The role of an animator** is to help a community discover and use all its potential for creative and constructive team work. The word means "one who gives new spirit and life to a group".

An animator needs all the skills of a facilitator but the animator also has a special responsibility to stimulate people:

- to think critically,
- to identify problems,
- to find new solutions.

The animator challenges the group to look at the causes and the consequences of the facts they are considering. For this (s)he may need a code to focus everyone's attention immediately on the same problem, and a careful plan to help the group move progressively from one step to the next.

The animator provides a process in which people can:
- share their concerns, their information, their opinions
- analyse the situation
- set goals
- make decisions
- plan action.

The animator, like the facilitator, needs to **understand the different forces** operating in a group. When the process gets stuck, the animator needs to identify the problem. It may be a hidden conflict, a lack of information, a power struggle, or some other problem.

The animator needs to enable the group to understand the problem and deal with it constructively.

Paulo Freire has summarised the differences between the role of a teacher in banking education and the role of an animator in problem-posing education.

| Banking education | Problem-posing education |
|---|---|
| • The teacher talks, passing on information.<br>• The pupils sit and listen quietly, and act passively. | • The animator poses the problem and asks questions.<br>• The participants are active, describe their experiences, share ideas, analyse and plan. |

Many of us have had very little experience in an educational process which is truly problem-posing, but we have all had much experience of "banking". We therefore have a tendency to move back very easily to the traditional "teaching method" if we do not design problem-posing learning events or meetings carefully.

**The role of a coordinator** is to draw together people, actions and events, in such a way that they support and strengthen each other, and do not compete or clash with each other. There needs to be coordination within each program and coordination between different programs. The role of the coordinator will be dealt with much more fully in Chapter 10, Book III.

**A group leader** can be any one of these types. The word "leader" is a vague term when we see how many different types of leadership there are and what is needed in a group. See Chapter 10 Book III, for further elaboration of different leadership styles.

# B. Content and process*

There are two important aspects of every discussion.

1. **What** the group is talking about – the content.
2. **How** the group talks about the subject – the process.

Process is a means to discuss content in the most fruitful way possible. The role of a facilitator is to provide a process which will help the group to discuss their content satisfactorily and productively.

The role of an animator is both to stimulate reflection and action on a particular issue and to provide a process for active and responsible participation.

Every group leader needs to understand clearly how the process affects the level of discussion on the content, and the commitment of the group to carrying out any decisions that may be made.

## 1. WHAT TO OBSERVE IN A GROUP

All of us have spent a good part of our lives in groups of various sorts, but rarely have we taken time to stop and observe what is going on in the group, why the members are behaving the way they are. It is difficult to observe and participate at the same time, and the skill of doing both at the same time can only be gained by practice.

**We need to observe at three different levels:**

a. **Content:** What is the group talking about?
What is each person saying?

b. **Non-verbal expressions:** Apart from what they say, what indications are people giving of their feelings and reactions. For example, gestures, tone of voice, body language, facial expressions, order of speaking, etc.

c. **Feelings, attitudes, concerns, hidden agendas**

These factors have an important effect on the life and work of a group and must be taken into account. Sensitive observation of the words and non-verbal expressions can give us clues about their feelings, but these clues can easily be misinterpreted, and so if they seem important they should be checked with the person concerned, e.g. "Are you feeling uncomfortable about that decision, Ngugi?"

---

* Episcopal Church, *Basic Reader in Human Relations Training*, Part I, pp. 41 & 42.

## Communication

One of the easiest aspects of group process is to observe the pattern of communication:

1.  Who talks?
    For how long?
    How often?
2.  Who do people look at when they talk?
    - Other individuals, possibly potential supporters?
    - Scanning the group?
    - No one?
    - The ceiling?
3.  Who talks after whom, or who interrupts whom?
4.  What style of communication is used
    - strong statements,
    - questions,
    - gestures,
    - laughter,
    - tears, etc.?

The kind of observations we make gives us clues to other important things which may be going on in the group, such as who leads whom, or who influences whom? The following exercises give people practice in observing group process.

## 2.  SOCIOGRAM

The sociogram can be used as a special exercise of observation, or it can be practised at any meeting, seminar or discussion. It is a simple chart showing who speaks to whom in a group, and how frequently each person speaks.

## Procedure 1

1.  The observers write the names of all the people in the group in the order in which they are sitting. It is best to draw a large circle for this.

X   Ngugi

Mary  X                    X  Jim

Anne  X

Peter  X                          X  John

Joseph  X

X  Kamau

Theresa  X        X  Mulwa

2.  Then as the discussion proceeds, draw a line each time a different person speaks. If the communication is direct from one person to another, draw a solid line with an arrow showing who speaks to whom. If the remark is made to the group in general, draw a dotted line to the middle of the circle.

   After observing a group for 15 – 20 minutes, the sociogram may look like this:

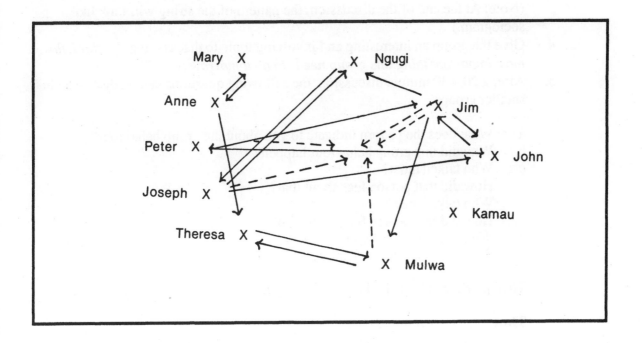

**Note:** In the above example, you can see women spoke only to women and men to men. This may be the case, but the point is to see the patterns of communication clearly and objectively through the chart. You can also see that Jim spoke most often and Kamau never spoke.

3.  Afterwards the observers show their charts to a small group. In small groups of 3 or 4 people with 1 or 2 observers in each group, discuss:

   a.  What patterns of communication do we see in the chart?

   b.  In what ways do these patterns help or hinder the life and work of the group?

## Summary

The insights can be shared in the whole group if appropriate. The sociogram may reveal some strong patterns of domination and, if so, the group needs to know how to give and receive feedback constructively. (See page 67 for this input.) The animator could also share with the group the reading on collective leadership by Cabral found earlier in this chapter.

### Procedure 2

1.  Instead of drawing a chart and asking people to observe a discussion, a ball of string can be used to record the pattern of a discussion.
2.  Ask participants to form mixed groups with 8 people in each group. Each group is given a ball of string which is put in the centre of their circle.
3.  Each time a person wishes to speak, they need to have the ball of string in their hands. As you speak, you tie the string around your pen/pencil once.
    (Note: At the end of the discussion, the pattern of the string will look like a sociogram.)
4.  Give the group an interesting and involving topic to discuss (e.g. *" I think the most important thing this group needs to do tomorrow is . . ."*)
5.  After a 20 – 30 minute discussion, the following questions can be discussed in smaller groups.

    a.  What does the pattern indicate to you about the group behaviour?
    b.  Why did this group behaviour happen?
    c.  Who talked most?
        How did that person feel about that?
    d.  Who talked least?
        How did that person feel about that?
    e.  What did I learn from this exercise?
        What does this suggest about our working together in the whole group?

6.  Then points can be shared in the whole group.

    **Time**      1 – 1½ hours

    **Materials** 1 ball of string for every 8 participants. Each person should have a pen or pencil.

## 3.    ROLE PLAY ON DIFFERENT LEADERSHIP STYLES

This exercise helps a group to see how the behaviour of the leader affects the group he or she is working with. It is a good exercise to use at the beginning of a workshop on leadership.

### Procedure

Either this can be prepared ahead of time and rehearsed (in which case it will be a skit and not a role play), or people who are familiar with the exercise can play the roles of the two different leaders and volunteers can be called for from the group to play the other roles.

(All these volunteers should realise that they are taking part in a role play in which particular roles will be played by the participants. If they enter into a serious decision-making process and later find that others are acting roles, they may feel they have been manipulated, and resent this.)

1.  About six volunteers should be called for, for each of the two plays. Each should be asked to act out a meeting of some group with which they are familiar, e.g. a school or development committee or a parish council. They are given a task to make a decision on some matter of general interest to the whole group (but not too absorbing an interest). If the group becomes too absorbed in the subject matter, they will not be able to reflect objectively on the leadership styles later.

2.  The first leader is told to act the part of a very **dictatorial** chairperson. S/he calls for ideas, but does not listen to people, squashes their suggestions, imposes his or her own point of view on the group, etc.

3.  Other members of the group are each given specific roles:
    a.  one is asked to support whatever the chairperson suggests,
    b.  another suggests several different possibilities,
    c.  another supports this speaker,
    d.  another interrupts and opposes the chairperson, etc.
    These instructions can either be given orally to individuals before doing the play, or be written on slips of papers for each volunteer.

4.  The chairs should be arranged in an open circle in front of the group so that everyone can see and hear well. The actors should be reminded to speak clearly and make all their gestures quite visible.

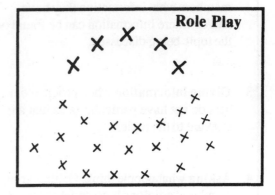

5.  The chairperson starts the play and each person participates in the role (s)he has been given.

6.  When the situation has become clear to the audience, the animator stops the action and asks the second group of six to come to the chairs.

7.  This is a different committee in a different place, but their task is similar. Most of the members have been given similar instructions about their roles, but this time the chairperson has been asked to be very **passive** (or laissez-faire – "let them do as they choose"). This leader shows little interest, makes no suggestions, does not respond to suggestions of the group, does not help to reach decisions or resolve conflict.

8.  Again the animator cuts the play when the situation has become clear.

9.  The animator then puts up four sheets of newsprint headed:
    a.  What did the 1st leader do in the group?
    b.  How did the group react?
    c.  What did the 2nd leader do in the group?
    d.  How did the group react?

10. If the group is fairly big, it is best to let the participants buzz about these questions in 3s for a few minutes before gathering up all the answers in the whole group.

11. After the mistakes and reactions have been fully discussed, the animator asks another question:
    e.g. "What does a good facilitator **do** in a group?"
    (Note: Here the group is asked to focus on what the facilitator does, e.g. "listens to each speaker with concentration", etc., not just the general moral virtues such as "the leader is kind and just".)

12. Finally the role play can be re-acted with someone who volunteers to play the part of a democratic chairperson as effectively as possible.

**Summary**

The animator may wish to summarise all the points made by the group and also add points on the role of an animator and a facilitator. (See pages 49 – 51 in this chapter.)

**Time**         About 1 – 1½ hours.

**Materials**    Moveable chairs for the play, newsprint, tape, and felt pens.

## TASK AND RELATIONSHIP NEEDS IN ANY GROUP

In every group, someone is needed to play each of the following roles if the group is to accomplish its task and keep good relationships among its members:

### TASK NEEDS

1. **Starting the discussion** or helping the group begin a job.

2. **Asking for information.** Asking group members what information they have and/or where information can be found on the topic being discussed.

3. **Giving information** when group members do not have particular facts that are relevant to the topic.

4. **Asking** what people think. Getting group members' opinions is essential for good decision-making. It is also important for people to be willing to share what they think.

5. **Explaining.** Giving practical examples to make a point clear.

6. **Summing up.** Repeating what has been said clearly in a few words.

7. **Checking** to see if everyone agrees.

8. **Analysing** the problems under discussion.

9. **Making creative suggestions** to resolve the problems.

10. **Having a clear process** for making each decision.

11. **Evaluating.** Looking at the strengths and weaknesses of the group's work and seeing how it can be improved.

### RELATIONSHIP NEEDS

1. **Encouraging.** Being friendly, responding to and building on suggestions made by others. Showing acceptance and appreciation of others and their ideas.

2. **Giving** everyone a chance to speak.

3. **Asking** what people feel. Sharing what one feels and checking group feelings (e.g. are people tired?).

4. **Encouraging** shy members, especially young women or those less formally schooled.

5. **Resolving** arguments.

6. **Encouraging** creativity in the group.

7. **Sharing** responsibilities.

8. **Developing the confidence** and skills of all members.

9. **Setting standards.** (e.g. "Shall we agree that nobody speaks more than twice?")

10. **Diagnosing difficulties.** (e.g. "Maybe some of us are afraid of the consequences of this decision.")

11. **Relieving tension.** By bringing it out into the open, putting a problem in a wider context, or making a well-timed joke.

The chairperson will fulfil some of these roles, but it is difficult for any one person to fulfil them all. It is good if the group can share responsibility for leadership by observing carefully which needs are not being attended to and calling attention to these needs, e.g. "Perhaps we need to get more information before we can make a decision", or "Perhaps we need a summary of the main points which have been made so far".

# C. Shared leadership*

If a group has just done the previous exercise, one can look back to the list made of what a good animator needs to do in the group. It usually strikes the group that this involves an awful lot for one person to concentrate on and that the animator needs help from the rest of the group. The following discussion can help a group to be much clearer about shared leadership and the role of the animator.

**Procedure**

1. When the group has just had a fairly positive experience of discussion and decision-making, ask them to form groups of 3s and discuss:
   *What factors helped the group to reach its goal?* Ask them to be as specific as possible, e.g. not just everyone was cooperative, but to explain in what way people were cooperative.

2. Make a list on newsprint of all the different factors mentioned. Then show most of these factors were meeting needs of one of two kinds:
   - Helping to **get the task completed,** or
   - Helping to **sustain the relationships and maintain a good spirit in the group.**

3. Draw a bicycle and list the task needs under the back wheel and the relationship needs under the front wheel. A bicycle is driven forward by the back wheel, to which the pedals and chain are attached. The back wheel represents the task needs, which push the group towards its goals. The front wheel controls the steering and balance of the bicycle, so this wheel represents the relationship needs of the group.

| **Task Needs** | **Relationship Needs** |
| --- | --- |
| _____ | _____ |
| _____ | _____ |
| _____ | _____ |
| _____ | _____ |

* Episcopal Church, *Basic Reader in Human Relations Training,* Part I, pp. 43, 44.

4.   Ask what happens in a group if:
     a.   the task needs are ignored
     b.   the relationship needs are ignored.
5.   Handout the prepared list of task and relationship functions (found on page 58) and ask them to compare this with their own list, noting anything missing.
6.   Explain then that leadership involves being sensitive to the needs of the group at any particular moment and responding to this need. This response can be given by any member of the group, not necessarily the chairperson or animator. **This then becomes shared leadership.**
7.   Draw the following diagram on the board and explain how leadership becomes shared over a period of time.

**Shared Leadership and Participation**

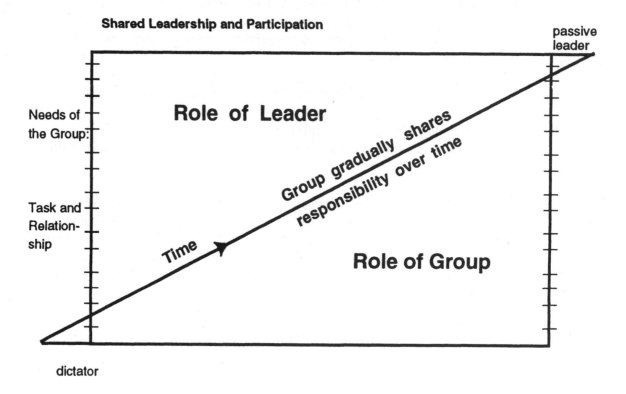

It takes time for a group to develop an effective way of sharing leadership. At first the leader may need to respond to as many of the needs as (s)he can her/himself. Members who have had training will quickly recognise group needs and start responding to these needs also.

As the group members get to know each other, gradually different members will assume more and more of the leadership roles themselves. The leader should then take responsibility mainly for those needs which no one else in the group seems to be meeting. This will vary from group to group. Sometimes the leader may notice that everyone is asking for or giving information very freely, but no one is gatekeeping. At other times group members may be full of original ideas but no one is summarising or building upon the ideas offered, etc.

As the group members take more responsibility for the life of the group, the leader can become less active. This process shows how a group becomes self-governing, self-reliant and not dependent.

# 1.   PO-PO (PARTICIPANT/OBSERVER EXERCISE)

This exercise can be used to practise shared leadership and gain insight into needs of a group through observation.

**Procedure**

1.   Ask the group to divide into two equal groups. Each group will have one turn working in the fishbowl and one turn observing.
2.   Group A is asked to go into the fishbowl (a circle of chairs in the middle). Each member of Group B is assigned a partner in Group A whom (s)he is to observe. They should sit in an outer circle opposite their partner so that they can see and hear well.
3.   An interesting topic, which involves both sharing of ideas and decision-making, is given, for example:
     "What do you feel are the main things hindering development in your area?" and "List the 3 most important things that this group could start to do about them."
4.   It is suggested that the group should not choose a chairperson but that each member of the group should try to fulfil the needs as they arise.
5.   The observers are asked to take notes on the needs they see in the  group, and the responses of the person they are observing.
6.   After 10 – 15 minutes' discussion, the animator breaks the group and each participant meets with his or her observer for 5 minutes of discussion and feedback on the process.
7.   The first group returns to the fishbowl to try to make their decisions in another 10 – 15 minutes.
8.   Both groups evaluate together how effectively Group A worked on the decisions and what else would have helped the group to work more effectively. It is important at this point to keep the discussion on the **process** and not return to the **content** of the discussion.
9.   The two groups now reverse roles: Group B go into the middle and Group A are the observers. A different, but comparable,  task is given to Group B and the same steps are followed.

**Note:**      Sometimes it is helpful to provide the observers with a form listing the Task and Relationship Needs, and to ask them to make a note each time they see a person fulfilling one of these needs.

This type of concentrated observation is important training in helping people to become much more aware of group process. It is usually not possible for us to do this when we are actively involved in discussing the content.

>    **Time**      Between 2 and 3 hours.

>    **Materials**  Paper, pencils,  forms for observers on task and relationship functions. The group should be about 16 –  24 people.

## 2. DRAWING A HOUSE

This exercise may be used to discuss cooperation and control in a group. Sometimes we think we are working with other people, when in fact we are controlling the whole process without realising it.

**Rules and directions**
- a. Choose a partner.
- b. Hold one pen or pencil together in such a way that you are able both to write and to draw with it.
- c. On the given piece of paper, both together draw a house and write a title for your drawing.
- d. All keep silent during the drawing and writing.

About five minutes are given for the explanation of the rules and the drawing.

**Discussion**
- e. Next, each pair who have drawn together, sit together for about 5 minutes and discuss:
  - i. What were your feelings and reactions during the exercise?
  - ii. What helped you and hindered you during the exercise?
- f. Next, two pairs come together to form a group of four and discuss:
  "How does this relate to our life and work together now?" Discuss this for about 15 minutes and then share in the whole group.

**Time** 30 – 45 minutes

**Materials** Pen and paper for each pair of participants.


## 3. MIRRORING

This light-hearted exercise is used to discuss feelings and attitudes in leading and following. A good evening session.

**Procedure**
- a. Each person chooses a partner and they stand facing each other with their hands up, a few inches apart. They imitate the movements of their partner like the reflection in a mirror, taking turns to lead and follow, according to their own timing.
- b. For the second round, the partners continue mirroring, but touch one another's hands lightly.
- c. In the third round, they are told to press their hands together hard, continuing to take turns to lead and follow.

**Discussion questions**

1. How were the 3 experiences different from each other for you?
2. How did you feel during each experience about leading and following?
3. What similarities do you find in the relationship between leader and follower in everyday life?

**Time** 30 – 45 minutes

**Material** Taped music can be used or silence.

## 4. KEEPING PARTICIPATION OPEN TO ALL

In the "heat" of a discussion, some people become very animated and unaware of their behaviour, not realising that they are speaking a lot of the time. In order to keep participation open, especially to those who are more quiet or "think before they speak", it helps to have a method of maintaining self-awareness as part of group life.

Two methods of helping a group to become conscious of who speaks, how often, and who is not getting an opportunity to speak, are included below:

**a. The talking stick**

There are many fine carved sticks in Africa. One of these can be used instead as a "talking stick". It can be placed in the middle of the room at the beginning of a discussion. Anyone who wishes to speak must pick up the stick and hold it while they are speaking. When someone else wants to speak, they signal that they want the stick. A younger person can be responsible for the stick and take it to anyone who shows they wish to speak, taking care not to ignore any requests, particularly of those who have not yet spoken.

**b. Beans**

Another procedure is to give every participant beans at the beginning of a discussion. Each time they speak they must throw a bean into the centre of the circle. They may not speak again in the group until all the others who wish to speak have had their chance. When a person has no beans left, (s)he no longer can speak.

## 5. WHAT METHODS HAVE WE USED SO FAR?

When people are using group methods, it is very important that they understand the reasons why a specific method is used at a particular time. If an animator does not know why (s)he is using a particular method, many mistakes and conflicts can arise. Learning these skills takes experience and sensitive judgment by the animator.

One becomes more sensitive through reflection. It can be useful to reflect on the workshop currently in process, to analyse the methods used and the reasons for using particular methods.

### Procedure

1. After 3 days (or at the end of a workshop) the following questions can be posed to the group.
   a. What different methods have been used during this workshop which have helped you to
      ● participate actively and
      ● think critically and creatively?

   b. What were the reasons behind the use of each method?

2. In the whole group, the animator can easily use this session to link the group learnings to relevant theories, such as developing trust, learning climate, use of small groups, etc, which can be found in Chapter 4.

**Time**          1$\frac{1}{2}$ to 3 hours depending on the depth of analysis.
**Materials**     None

---

## Self´ and mutual criticism

Amilcar Cabral, the founder of the PAIGC in Guinea Bissau, wrote of the need for self´ and mutual criticism in any effective movement or political party.

Develop the spirit of criticism between leaders and members. "Give everyone at every level the opportunity to criticise, to give their opinion about the work and the behaviour, and the action of others. Accept criticism, wherever it comes from, as a contribution to improving the work . . .

"Always remember that criticism is not to speak **ill** nor to engage in intrigues. Criticism is and should be the act of expressing an open, candid opinion in front of those concerned, on the basis of facts and in a spirit of fairness, to assess the thought and action of others, with the aim of improving that thought and action. Criticism is to be constructive, to show proof of sincere interest in the work of others, for the improvement of that work.

"Combat severely the **evil tongue,** the obsession with intrigues, the 'so-and-so says', unfair and unfounded criticism. To assess the thought and action of a person is not necessarily to speak ill of it. To speak highly, to praise, to encourage, to stimulate – this is also criticism. While we must always be watchful against conceit and personal pride, we must not stint praise to someone who deserves it . . .

"Derive a lesson from every mistake we make or which others make, in order to avoid making new mistakes, so that we do not fall into the follies into which others have already fallen. Criticising a person does not mean putting oneself against the person, making a **sacrifice** in which the person is the victim: it is to show the person that we are all interested in the work, that we are all one and the same body . . . we must be capable of criticising and of accepting criticism.

"But criticism must be complemented by self-criticism, proof of our own willingness to help ourselves to improve our thoughts and our actions."

Amilcar Cabral
*Unity and Struggle,* p. 246

# D. Self and mutual criticism

## 1. JOHARI'S WINDOW*

This theory is a good introduction to any exercise on feedback. Each person is a mystery, partly known and partly unknown. The window, designed by Joe Luft and Harry Ingham, helps us to understand how we can grow in self-knowledge and how we can build deeper trust in teams and communities by sharing and feedback.

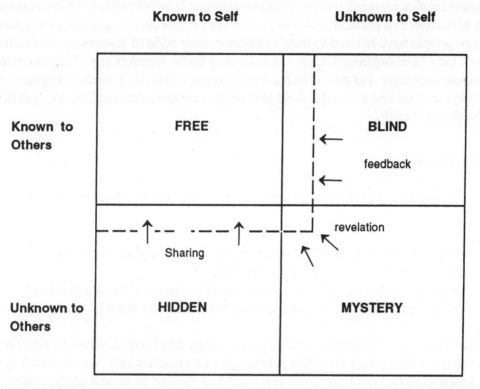

**The window represents the self – the whole person. The four panes of the window can be described as follows:**

**Free**      The part of yourself which is known to you and to others. It is the area of mutual sharing.

**Hidden**   That part of yourself which is known to you, but not shared with others. What is hidden may best remain hidden. But also it might clear the air, and build trust and make teamwork easier if more of yourself were known and shared.

**Blind**    That part of you which is known to others, but unknown to you. The tone of your voice, a conflict in which you are involved, a good trait of which you are not aware – all may be in this area.

**Mystery**  That part of yourself which is unknown to others and also unknown to you. Here are talents and abilities which you do not yet know you have and others have never seen. But they are part of you nevertheless, and may one day come to the surface.

---

\* Reprinted from *Group Processes: An Introduction to Group Dynamics* (1970) by Joseph Luft, by permission of Mayfield Publishing Company, Copyright © 1963, 1970 by Joseph Luft.

FEEDBACK

**Feedback**   is one way by which others open up to you the blind area of yourself by letting you know what they see in you which you do not see yourself.

**Sharing**   is one way of opening yourself more to others.

**Revelation** is an experience during which part of the mysterious area of yourself is suddenly revealed. Revelation comes spontaneously; it cannot be planned.

## Personal Feedback

Personal feedback means receiving information on how other people have reacted to one's own behaviour in a particular situation. It is very important for animators to know honestly how people have reacted to their behaviour, their style of leadership, and to the programs which they have organised. Only then can they know whether any changes or improvements are necessary. Far too often leaders continue organising certain programs, acting in certain ways, and no one ever tells them that people are not interested, or are "put off" by some of the things they do.

## Indirect Feedback

If we are sensitive we can pick up a great deal of indirect feedback through observation.

- Do people begin to look out of the window or get a glassy stare in their eyes after we have been speaking for some time?
- Do people quietly drop out of our meetings, classes, clubs or churches?
- Do groups actually carry out the plans we make with them?

However, if we rely on indirect feedback we may misinterpret what we observe. (Maybe someone with a glassy stare has actually got a stomachache!) We are much better off if we can ask people directly for their reactions and receive an honest reply, although sometimes people will fear to say exactly what they thought and felt if it was somewhat negative.

## Direct Feedback

The purpose of personal feedback is to improve a person's performance and build up their self-confidence. It is **totally unhelpful** just to cut a person down and destroy their self-confidence.

If it is well given and well received, feedback supports and encourages the helpful aspects of a person's behaviour and gives them an opportunity to change those aspects which are not helpful.

Direct and indirect personal feedback is different in different cultures. If we agree that improvement of one's work with people is essential, then the following exercises and inputs need to be adapted to each local culture.

> **One camel does not make fun of the other camel's hump**
> – Guinea

**Points to remember when giving feedback**

a. We can only give feedback helpfully to a person if they know that we accept and appreciate them as a person.

b. It is important that an atmosphere of trust and mutual appreciation be established when feedback is given. This can only exist if we give genuine and positive, as well as negative, feedback.

c Feedback should only be given if the person wants to know how others see him/her and has asked for feedback. It should be offered, not forced upon a person.

d. Feedback should deal with what a person **did,** their behaviour, not their motivation.

e. It is often best if we can present negative feedback as our own problem, a sharing of our personal feelings when something happened. For example, "I felt squashed and humiliated when you interrupted and brushed aside my suggestion just now", not "You always try to make people feel they have nothing to contribute". (Only the person concerned really knows why they acted as they did.)

f. Each person should express only their feelings and not assume that the whole group felt that way. Others can say so for themselves if they did.

g. Feedback should deal with things that can be changed. "I would find it easier to listen if you made fewer points at one time." Not "Your accent drives me mad" or, "I do not like the shape of your ears".

**Some points to remember in receiving feedback**

1. We learn most from feedback if we listen carefully to the feelings expressed and
   a. do not try to defend our behaviour or
   b. give reasons about why we acted in a particular way.

   One cannot argue with feelings. If a person felt bored or irritated or humiliated, it is no good telling them that "they ought not to have felt that way". Each person is the "expert" on their own feelings. Only by listening carefully to their analysis of what caused these feelings of boredom, irritation or humiliation, can an animator learn how to avoid boring, irritating or humiliating other people in the future.

2. A person receiving feedback always has the right to decide when (s)he has had enough for the time being. Just say, "OK. Thanks very much. I will think about all that, but I think it would be good to move on to someone or something else now."

3. A person who receives negative feedback should remember that different people react differently to different behaviour. (S)he may like to check how others reacted to the same thing. If only one person reacted negatively, (s)he might decide to do nothing about it, but if the entire group felt the same way, (s)he might realise that it is important to try and change that behaviour.

---

**Feedback plays an important role in team-building**

---

It helps ensure that everyone is able to make their best contribution, and helps to remove points of friction. It helps each person to know where (s)he stands and, if constructive suggestions are given, it soon builds solidarity and trust in the group.

---

He who cannot dance will say:
"The drum is bad."
                    – Ashanti

---

## 2.    MULTIPLE ROLE EXERCISE

This exercise helps people become more aware of their own behaviour in groups, and understand various types of behaviour in others. Recognising such differences can help a group and prepare people for feedback later.

**Procedure**

a.  Before you begin this exercise, have the following types of behaviour written on separate large pieces of paper:
    aggressive
    thoughtful – quiet
    task centred
    emotional
    rational (intellectual)

b.  The animator explains that there are many kinds of behaviour in groups and this exercise helps us understand the effects of our own behaviour and that of others in a group.

c.  (S)he explains that (s)he will put five pieces of paper around the room which describe five common kinds of behaviour. Each person is to consider these five kinds of behaviour and go and stand under the one that describes his or her usual behaviour in groups. They should not think too long about this, but move to the one that first strikes them as their most usual behaviour.

d.  The animator puts up the 5 types of behaviour, acting each one out as (s)he explains it. They should be put on different walls of the room, as far apart as possible.

e.  The animator then asks everyone to get up and go to the one which best describes themselves. If someone really cannot choose (which is unusual), they should sit in another place and talk with others who also cannot choose.

f.  Once people are standing under these signs, the animator asks them to form small groups of 3s to discuss: *"What is helpful about this kind of behaviour in groups, and what is not helpful?"*

g.  After about 10 minutes, the animator asks the participants to form a large circle again but to sit together with those who chose the same type of behaviour under their own signs.

h.  Each group then shares the helpful and not helpful sides of their own behaviour. There is usually much laughter but the animator needs to help the group not to defend their own behaviour and not to attack others' behaviour too much. In all the fun, help the group to recognise that we need all kinds of behaviour in a group to work well together.

**Time**         About 45 minutes to 1 hour.

**Materials**    The five types of behaviour written on 5 separate sheets of paper beforehand.

## 3.   STRENGTHEN TEAM RELATIONS

This exercise provides an opportunity for team members to give and receive helpful suggestions from each other for improving their team work.

**Procedure**

a.  Explain the purpose and the procedure of the exercise to the team. Then ask anyone who would like to receive feedback to volunteer to start the ball rolling by asking the others to tell him or her:
    1.  *What do I appreciate about your contribution and behaviour in the team?*
    2.  *What do I find difficult?*
    3.  *What I would like to request of you to make your teamwork more fruitful.*

b.  The person receiving feedback should call on those who show that they want to speak. This helps to make sure that people speak directly to the person concerned. "I really appreciate the fact that you are always ready to volunteer to take on jobs that need to be done . . ."

c.  If people start to speak about others, e.g. "Joe is very generous about volunteering, etc.", the animator should remind them to speak directly to the person concerned. As soon as everyone who wants to respond to a particular person has had an opportunity to do so, ask if anyone else wishes to hear reactions from the rest of the group.

d.  As far as possible, the group should avoid putting pressure on people to receive feedback. If they do not want it, they will not be able to use it constructively.

However, there are times when tension in a group becomes so acute that it becomes essential to deal with it if the group is to continue working as a team. At this point it may be necessary to challenge someone who does not usually invite feedback to have a frank discussion of the problems.

### Alternative questions

a.  What I see as your strengths as a member of the team.
b.  Some suggestions for using your gifts and skills more effectively on the team.

**OR**

c.  What I would like you to continue to do.
d.  What I would like you to stop doing.
e.  What I would like you to start doing.

## 4.  TEAM EFFECTIVENESS QUESTIONNAIRES*

Sometimes a team does not have much time for a long feedback session. However, it is important from time to time to check how well people are working together. These two questionnaires can be useful to find the areas of teamwork that need specific discussion.

### Procedure

a.  Have each person in the team or group fill out the questionnaire. This can take about 5 – 10 minutes.
b.  As a team, look at each question and see which points are rated low by all and which points have the greatest differences. These will be the areas about which the team needs to have clear and frank discussions.

---

* Episcopal Church, *Basic Readers in Human Relations Training,* Part VIII, pp. 84 — 86.

## Team effectiveness questionnaire – task needs

**Directions:** Place a check mark along each line (scale), showing where you would rate your team. Discuss your relations with your team. Where there are differences, try to clarify what you need to do to help the team work better.

### Task Functions

1. How clear are the **goals** of this team?

| 0 | 1 | 2 | 3 | 4 | 5 | 6 | 7 |
|---|---|---|---|---|---|---|---|

| Utter confusion | Clear to a few | | Fairly clear to most now | | | Clear focus, shared by all. | |

2. How strongly **involved** do we feel in what this team is doing?

| 0 | 1 | 2 | 3 | 4 | 5 | 6 | 7 |
|---|---|---|---|---|---|---|---|

| Couldn't care less | | Not much interested | | | Interested | Deeply involved | |

3. How well do we **diagnose** our team problems?

| 0 | 1 | 2 | 3 | 4 | 5 | 6 | 7 |
|---|---|---|---|---|---|---|---|

| Avoid, pretend they do not exist | Slight attention | | | Considerable attention | | Face frankly, analyse with care | |

4. How appropriate are our ways of working and **procedures** for our team goals?

| 0 | 1 | 2 | 3 | 4 | 5 | 6 | 7 |
|---|---|---|---|---|---|---|---|

| Defeating our purpose | Not much help | | | Often seem useful | | The best possible means to our ends | |

5. How well do we **integrate** contributions from various members?

| 0 | 1 | 2 | 3 | 4 | 5 | 6 | 7 |
|---|---|---|---|---|---|---|---|

| Each goes it alone, disregards others, no summary or integration | Slight attention to others' ideas | | | Considerable attention to using ideas of others | | Each speaks, builds directly on others' points | |

6. How do we usually make **decisions?**

| 0 | 1 | 2 | 3 | 4 | 5 | 6 | 7 |
|---|---|---|---|---|---|---|---|

| We do not | One-person decision taken as consent | Two people | Minority | Majority | Pressur-ed agree-ment | True con-sensus | |

7. How fully do we use **the resources** and creativity of our members for accomplishing goals?

| 0 | 1 | 2 | 3 | 4 | 5 | 6 | 7 |
|---|---|---|---|---|---|---|---|

| No one con-tributes freely, resources unused | Only a few contribute | | Most members contribute a great deal | | | Everyone contributes fully and creatively | |

## Group effectiveness questionnaire – relationship needs

**Directions:** Place a tick mark along each line, showing where you would rate this team at this time. Discuss your reactions with your team. Where there are differences, try to clarify what you need to do to help the team work better.

**Relationship functions**

1. How much do members enjoy working with the others in the team?

| 0 | 1 | 2 | 3 | 4 | 5 | 6 | 7 |
|---|---|---|---|---|---|---|---|
| All hate it, ready to quit | | Discontented | Some pleased, some don't care, some displeased | | Rather pleased, some enjoyment | All love it, real joy, active co-operation | |

2. How much encouragement, support and appreciation do we give to one another as we work?

| 0 | 1 | 2 | 3 | 4 | 5 | 6 | 7 |
|---|---|---|---|---|---|---|---|
| None | Seldom give support | | Some appreciated, some ignored, some criticised | | Often give support | Abundant for every member even when we disagree | |

3. How freely are our personal and group feelings expressed?

| 0 | 1 | 2 | 3 | 4 | 5 | 6 | 7 |
|---|---|---|---|---|---|---|---|
| No feelings expressed, all work-centred | Seldom express feelings, only negative or only positive ones | | Feelings expressed when unusually strong | | Often express feelings, positive and negative | Both personal and group feelings expressed | |

4. How constructively are we able to use disagreement and conflicts in team?

| 0 | 1 | 2 | 3 | 4 | 5 | 6 | 7 |
|---|---|---|---|---|---|---|---|
| Avoid or repress them. So bad they could break up the group | Seldom examine conflicts | | Smooth them over, change the subject or occasional constructive exploration | | Often explore conflicts | Welcome them, explore them, find them most valuable | |

5. How sensitive and responsive are we to the feelings of others which are not being explicitly expressed?

| 0 | 1 | 2 | 3 | 4 | 5 | 6 | 7 |
|---|---|---|---|---|---|---|---|
| Blind, insensitive, unconcerned | Seldom notice them | | Occasional response to such feelings | | Often respond to them | Fully aware, very sensitive, very responsive | |

## 5.    ANIMAL CODES – UNHELPFUL BEHAVIOUR IN A GROUP

We all delight in hearing we have been helpful in a group, but it is hard to face honestly the fact that some of our behaviour has not been helpful. This exercise uses humour to make this easier.

It should only be used after a group has been together for some time and when hard work in groups has broken down the first politeness, and participants have shown some of their characteristic reactions in time of stress. We have given 18 different animals to illustrate different behaviours. Some of them at first glance seem like the same behaviour (e.g. running away or withdrawing from conflict). There is a subtle difference. Feel free to pick and choose the animals you think are relevant or choose different animals to suit your own culture.

### Procedure

1.    The animator explains that we need to look at the negative as well as the positive side if we are to improve our leadership skills. Animals show in a very clear way some kinds of human behaviour.

2.    The animator(s) describe with actions, gestures and humour each type of behaviour, and then they put up a picture of the animal described.

### The Donkey
who is very stubborn, will not change his/her point of view.

### The Lion
who gets in and fights whenever others disagree with his/her plans or interfere with her/his desires.

### The Rabbit
who runs away as soon as (s)he senses tension, conflict, or an unpleasant job. This may mean quickly switching to another topic (flight behaviour).

### The Ostrich
who buries his or her head in the sand and refuses to face reality or admit there is any problem at all.

73

Fooling and joking

**The Monkey**
who fools around, chatters a lot and prevents the group from concentrating on any serious business.

"Blocks - I won't let you go down this road."

**The Elephant**
who simply blocks the way, and stubbornly prevents the group from continuing along the road to their desired goal.

"Above it all"

**The Giraffe**
who looks down on the others, and the program in general, feeling, "I am above all this childish nonsense."

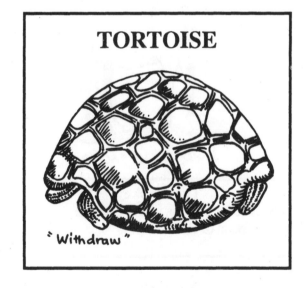

"Withdraw"

**The Tortoise**
who withdraws from the group, refusing to give his or her ideas or opinions.

**The Cat**

who is always looking for sympathy. "It is so difficult for me... mia<u>o</u>w . . ."

**The Peacock**

who is always showing off, competing for attention. "See what a fine fellow I am!"

**The Snake**

who hides in the grass and strikes unexpectedly.

**The Rhino**

who charges around "putting her/his foot in it", and upsetting people unnecessarily.

**The Owl**

who looks very solemn and pretends to be very wise, always talking in long words and complicated sentences.

**The Mouse**

who is too timid to speak up on any subject.

**The Frog**
who croaks on and on about the same subject in a monotonous voice.

**The Hippo**
who sleeps all the time, and never puts up his head except to yawn.

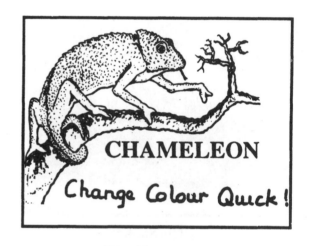

**The Fish**
who sits there with a cold glassy stare, not responding to anyone or anything.

**The Chameleon**
who changes colour according to the people she is with. She'll say one thing to this group and something else to another.

3.  After each animal has been explained and the pictures put up, the participants are asked to find a partner with whom they feel at home and discuss:
    *"If and when they have behaved like any one of these animals during the workshop?"*

4.  Later these animals provide the group with a helpful vocabulary for giving feedback to one another. This should not be imposed upon people but only given if it is requested.

**Time**    About 45 minutes.

**Materials**   Pictures of animals.

## 6. PARENT–ADULT–CHILD

This exercise is based on a pyschological theory called Transactional Analysis, developed by Eric Berne. A fuller explanation of it can be found in the book *I'm OK, You're OK* by Dr. Harris. A transaction is an exchange between two people, where one says or does something and the other responds.

Briefly it recognises that no matter how old we are, there are within each one of us three different modes of being.

**The Child**    reacting spontaneously, instinctively, and emotionally to any experience. The child is sometimes free and joyful, sometimes submissive, fearful, or stubborn.

**The Parent**    conditioned by the training we received in childhood from our parents and other authority figures, to react from a sense of obligation and duty. "You must", "You should", "You ought to", etc. The parent is sometimes caring and understanding, sometimes harsh and critical.

**The Adult**    making independent judgments, looking for reasons, seeking alternative solutions in difficult situations. (This "adult" starts developing in a person from the age of 10 months.)

Each of us reacts to different situations sometimes as a child, sometimes as a parent, and sometimes as an adult, and the way we react often brings out the opposite reaction in the other person. E.g. if we behave like a parent, we often draw out a childish emotional reaction from the other. If we behave like a child, we push the other into the role of the parent. If we behave like an adult, we draw out the adult in the other person as well.

Each of these modes is appropriate at certain times and inappropriate at others. Each has both positive and negative forms. For example,

- the laughing child having fun, and the whining self-pitying child,
- the caring, protective parent, and the critical, know-all parent,
- the thoughtful, responsible adult, and the over-serious worker who cannot relax.

### Procedure A

The aim of this exercise is to help people become more aware of when they are behaving in each of these ways and the effect it is having on other people. It has been helpful in dealing with husband–wife, priest–catechist, teacher–pupil communication (give other examples of whomever the group can identify with).

**CODE**  A short play involving two young adults (either both men or both women or a married couple) who share a room at a conference or some place that is familiar to the group.

### Scene 1:    The Child

It is 8 in the morning. 'A' returns from the shower knowing (s)he is late. (S)he starts looking for her or his watch and starts throwing things all over the place as (s)he cannot find it. (S)he gets angrier and angrier, crying or swearing. Finally the person sweeps the watch onto the floor while searching through a shelf, and it gets broken. This makes the person even more furious. (Stop the play here.)

### Discussion questions

1. What did you notice about the behaviour of this person?
2. Either in 3s or in the whole group, participants discuss this question and then the animator makes a list on newsprint of the behaviour mentioned. After this brief discussion, the animator puts a picture of a child and lets the group comment on it.

### Scene 2:   The Parent

It is now 6 in the evening. The second actor, 'B', comes home from work and starts looking for some money (s)he left somewhere. (S)he also starts getting emotional and making a mess, similar to the first scene. 'A' comes in and starts scolding 'B'. "You ought to put your money away more carefully," etc. The more person 'A' scolds, the more angry and unreasonable 'B' becomes. (Stop the play here.)

### Discussion questions

1. What did you notice about B's behaviour?
2. What did you notice about A's behaviour?

The animator makes a list of the behaviour of the "parent" on newsprint. After a brief discussion, the animator puts up a picture of the parent and lets the group comment.

### Scene 3:    The adult

A week later 'A' comes home from work and starts looking for a letter from a friend which he or she wants to answer. (S)he cannot find it. 'B' comes in and asks what the trouble is. When 'A' explains, 'B' starts to help look, and ask questions, "When can you last remember seeing it? Where were you sitting?", etc.

Both try to think through the whole process carefully and reasonably.  Suddenly 'A' remembers (s)he  was reading a particular book, finds  that book and, behold, there is the letter inside the book.

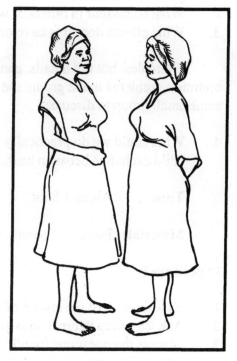

### Discussion questions

1.    What  did you notice about the behaviour of each  person in this play?

2.    The animator writes their points on newsprint.

After a number of suggestions, the animator puts up the picture of two adults, discussing as equals, looking each other in the eyes, etc.

After comments s/he draws the following diagram and explains how different transactions can take place.

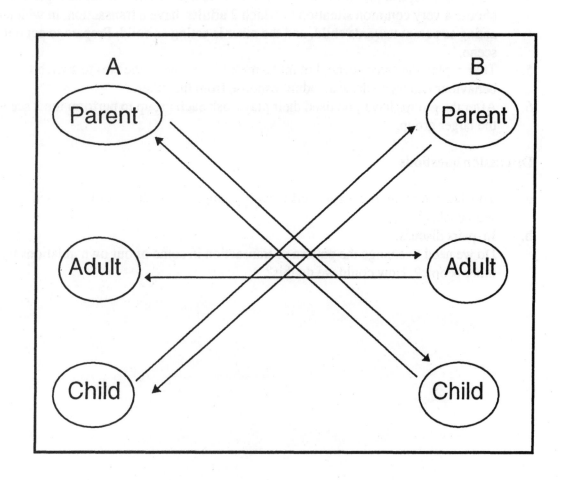

## Final discussion

The group is asked to go into 2s or 3s (with people they trust) and to discuss:

1. What situations can they recall in which they personally have felt or acted like a child, parent, or an adult?
2. What behaviour in others or what situations bring this out in themselves?
3. What effects does this have on the other involved?

Examples, but not details, can be shared in the whole group. If there are one or more common problems in the group, the participants could continue by getting back into the same small group to discuss:

4. What could we do practically to develop an adult–adult exchange instead of a parent–child exchange between husband and wife, or priest and catechist, etc.

**Time**     About 1 hour.

**Materials**  Posters of parent, child, adult; newsprint, markers, tape.

## Procedure B

1. Explain each of the modes of behaviour, putting up the poster of each as you do so.
2. Ask the group to break into groups of 2 or 3, choosing people they know and trust.
3. Discuss the questions found in the final discussion in the previous exercise.
4. Ask two groups to join together to form 4s or 5s and then ask these new groups to choose a very common situation in which 2 **adults** have a transaction, in which one is acting as parent towards child, and the other is acting as child. Prepare to act out this scene.
5. Then replay the same scene, but in the middle, get one of the two to switch to adult behaviour and try to draw an adult response from the other.
6. After the groups have practised their plays, ask each group to perform the 2 scenes for the larger group.

## Discussion questions

a. To what extent did the players effectively change to an adult–adult transaction in the second play?
b. In pairs discuss:
   Do we need to change the pattern of transaction in some of our own relationships with other people? How could we do this?

## The spirit of self-criticism

"[Develop] the spirit of self-criticism: the ability of each person to make specific analysis of his or her own work, to distinguish in it what is good from what is bad, to acknowledge our own errors and to discover the causes and the effects of these errors. To make self-criticism is not merely to say, 'Yes, I recognise my fault, my error and I ask for forgiveness,' while remaining ready soon to commit new faults, new errors. It is not pretending to be repentant of the evil one has done, while remaining convinced deep down that it is the others who do not understand. Still less is making self-criticism to make a ceremony so as to go on later with a clear conscience and carry on committing errors.

"Self-criticism is an act of frankness, courage, comradeship and awareness of our responsibilities, a proof of our will to accomplish and to accomplish properly . . . To criticise oneself is to reconstruct oneself within oneself in order to serve better."

Amilcar Cabral,
*Unity and Struggle*, p. 247

# E. Exercises on cooperation

## 1. JIGSAW COW

The aim of this exercise is to show the importance of cooperation in a group. The animator prepares a puzzle by cutting the pictures of two cows (one white and one black cow) into small pieces like a jigsaw puzzle.

**Procedure**

a. Divide the group into two smaller groups. Give out all the pieces of the white cow to one group. Give the other group all the pieces of the black cow except two, which the animator quietly steals and hides.

b. Explain that each piece is a piece of meat from the cow and each group must put their pieces together to make one complete cow.

c. The first group will finish quickly because they have all the pieces. The second group will probably struggle for a long time, and may call others to help. When they realise that some parts are missing, they will start searching for them.

d. Eventually they should find them in the pocket of the animator, and then they can fix the cow. The animator then stops the game and asks the following questions.

**Discussion questions**

1. What were you doing during the game?
2. Why did the first group finish before the second?
3. How did the second group feel
   a. when they could not complete the cow?
   b. when they found the pieces in the animator's pocket?
4. Do you ever see anything like this happening in real life? Give examples.
5. How do others feel if one person fails to make any contribution in a meeting or in a work project?
6. What are the results of some people contributing nothing?
7. What can we do to prevent this happening in our group?

**Time**    About 1 – 1¹/2 hours.

**Materials**    Two pictures of cows cut into pieces.

## 2.    BUILD WITH WHAT YOU'VE GOT

This exercise helps a group to look at problems of cooperation and communication. It can be great fun (sometimes also frustrating) and good for an evening activity.

### Procedure

a.    Before the exercise, the group leaders need to collect boxes of assorted odd-ments, filled with such things as old pieces of cloth, coloured paper, pipes, tools, sticks, bottles, etc. Each box should contain about 15 or more items and each box should be different from other boxes. You need to make one box for every 5 or 6 participants.

b.    When you begin the exercise, you explain that one of the difficulties in develop-ment (youth groups, etc.) is putting cooperation into practice. Rather than having an abstract discussion on cooperation, we will try to cooperate.

c.    Ask the participants to divide into groups of 5 or 6 people (only) and to stand around one of the tables in the room. Then give each group a box full of rubbish.

d.    The instructions for the exercise are then given:

1.    Each group has a box of things, and the task of each group is to build something that has **meaning** – it can be a symbol or something real.

2.    The group must work in **silence** (without words or writing notes to each other). They have to find other ways of communicating with each other.

3.    They can bring things from outside the box to add to their creation, if they want to.

4.    A prize will be given to the group that builds the most creative and clear thing (this can be a box of biscuits or something that the winners can share).

5.    They have 15 minutes to complete the task.

e.    After giving instructions and answering any questions, give the signal to begin work.

f.    After 15 minutes (or when it seems most groups have finished) stop the exercise.

g.    Ask everyone to go around and look at each thing that has been built, seeing if they can recognise what it is.

h.    Then have a vote by clapping. No group can clap for its own production but all others can clap. The group that gets the loudest clapping wins the prize.

### Discussion questions

1.    What helped cooperation in your group?

2.    What hindered cooperation in your group?
Were there times when you felt frustrated? Why did you feel so? What could the group have done to help you work better in the group?

3.    What have you learnt about cooperation?

4.    Did leadership emerge in the group at any point?
What type of leadership was helpful?

5.    At what point did the aim of the group become clear?
What effect did this have on cooperation?

6.    Do these things also happen in real life? How?

7.    In what ways can these difficulties be overcome?

The questions 1– 5 can be answered in the small groups.

In the large group, each group can report back on question number 3 and then the group leader can ask questions 6 and 7, putting on newsprint the points of questions number 3 and 7 only.

**Time**     About 1 hour.

**Materials**  Boxes full of rubbish as described at the beginning of this exercise. One box for every 5 or 6 participants. Newsprint, tape, felt pens.

## 3.    COOPERATIVE SQUARES EXERCISE*

This exercise helps a group to analyse some of the elements of co-operation, in order to look at their own behaviour when working in a group. It is a good exercise for an evening activity. (It is best to use the exercise with people who have a similar formal educational background. This exercise is based on geometry and some people who have little formal education may find the game too difficult. Then it can re-inforce their feeling of 'not being educated'.)

**Procedure**

1.    The animator begins by explaining that we want to look at what is essential to successful group co-operation.
2.    Ask the participants to form groups of five and to sit around a table. (It is possible to have one extra person to observe each group.)
3.    The animator then reads the instructions to the whole group.

**Instructions:**  Each of you will have an envelope which has pieces of cardboard for forming squares. When the animator gives the signal to begin, the task of your group is to form **five squares of equal size**. The task will not be completed until each has before him or her a perfect square of the same size as those in front of the other group members.

**Rules:**

a.    No member may speak. The task must be done in silence.
b.    You **may not take** or ask for a piece from any other person but you **can give** pieces to others.

4.    Ask if there are any questions and answer them.
5.    Give each group of five a set of squares in the five envelopes.
6.    Ask the groups to begin work. The animator watches the tables during the exercise to enforce the rules.
7.    When the task is completed, ask each group to discuss the following questions.

---

* Originally called *Broken Squares*, adapted from *Structured Experiences for Human Relations Training*, Vol. I, edited by J. William Pfeiffer and John E. Jones, University Associates, P.O. Box 80637, San Diego, CA. 92128, USA.

**Discussion questions**

    a.    In what way do you think each of you helped or hindered the group in completing its task?

    b.    How did members feel when someone holding a key piece did not see the solution?

    c.    How did members feel when someone completed a square incorrectly and then sat back without helping the group further?

    d.    What feelings did they think that person had?

    e.    How did members feel about the person who could not see the solution as quickly as others?

    f.    How are some of the things you learnt from this game true of real life and problems you have in your own situation?

After these questions are discussed in small groups, call the whole group together for a discussion on question f. Add a final question for the whole group.

    g.    What have we learnt about co-operation?

This question can be discussed in groups of 3s and then shared; points can be put up on newsprint.

**Summary**

Some points that may arise from the group can be summarised by the animator as follows:

    a.    Each person should understand the total problem.

    b.    Each person needs to understand how to contribute towards solving the problem.

    c.    Each person needs to be aware of the potential contributions of other members in a group.

    d.    When working co-operatively in groups, we need to recognise the problems of other people in order to help them make their maximum contribution.

    e.    Groups whose members pay attention to helping each other work well are likely to be more effective than groups whose members ignore each other.

**Variation**

If you have observers or if one group is having real difficulty in finishing the task, the observer or a member from a different group can tap someone in the group having difficulty and take their place. However, that person can refuse the 'aid' if they do not want help.

**Time**      About 1—1½ hours

**Materials**  A room with enough tables and chairs. Sets of broken squares made up for the number of participants in the group, newsprint, tape, felt pens.

## Directions for making a set of broken squares

A set consists of five envelopes containing pieces of cardboard cut into different patterns which, when properly arranged, will form five squares of equal size. One set should be provided for each group of five persons.

To prepare a set, cut out five cardboard squares, each exactly 6"x 6". Place the squares in a row and mark them as below, pencilling the letters lightly so they can be erased.

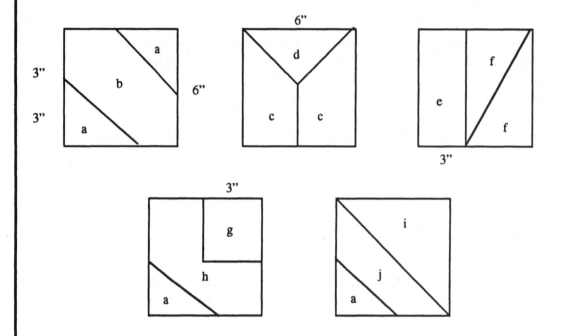

The lines should be so drawn that when cut out, all pieces marked 'a' will be exactly the same size, all pieces marked 'c' the same size, and so on. By using several combinations, two squares can be formed, but only one combination will form all five squares, each 6" x 6". After drawing the lines on the squares and labelling the sections with letters, cut each square along the lines into smaller pieces to make the parts of the puzzle.

Mark each of five envelopes A, B, C, D, and E. Distribute the cardboard pieces in the five envelopes as follows:

> Envelope A has pieces, i, h, e
> Envelope B has pieces, a, a, a, c
> Envelope C has pieces a, j
> Envelope D has pieces d, f
> Envelope E has pieces g, b, f, c

Erase the pencilled letter from each piece and write, instead, the appropriate envelope letter, as Envelope A, Envelope B, etc. This will make it easy to return the pieces to the proper envelope for subsequent use another time.

## 4. COMPETITION OR COOPERATION?*

The aims of this exercise are to explore trust between group members, the effects of betrayal of that trust, the effects of competition and the process of developing cooperation.

### Procedure

a.   Explain to the group that the purpose of the exercise is for each team **to get a positive score.** This must be stressed and written on newsprint for all to see.

b.   Two teams are formed and named Red and Blue. The teams are seated apart from each other. They are instructed not to communicate with the other team in any way, verbally or non-verbally, except when told to do so by the animator.

c.   The Red Team is given a card marked 'A' and one marked 'B'. The Blue Team is given a card marked 'X' and one marked 'Y'.

d.   Score sheets are distributed to all participants. They are given time to study the directions. The animator then asks if there are any questions concerning the scoring.

e.   Round One is begun. The animator tells the teams that they will have 3 minutes to make a team decision. (S)he instructs them not to write their decisions until given a signal that time is up. This is so that they will not make hasty decisions.

f.   The two teams are asked to hold up at the same moment the cards they have chosen. The scoring for that round is agreed upon and is entered on the score cards and on newsprint.

g.   Round 2 and 3 are conducted in the same way as Round 1.

h.   **First negotiation:** Round 4 is announced as a special round, for which the payoff points are doubled. Each team is instructed to send one representative to the chairs in the centre of the room. After representatives have conferred for three minutes, they return to their teams. Teams then have 3 minutes, as before, in which to make their decisions. When recording their scores, they should be reminded that points indicated by the payoff schedule are doubled for this round only.

i.   Rounds 5 through 8 are conducted in the same manner as the first 3 rounds.

j.   **Second negotiation:** Round 9 is announced as special round, in which the payoff points are 'squared' (multiplied by themselves, e.g. a score of 4 would be 4 x 4 = 16). A minus sign should be retained. e.g. $-3 \times -3 = -9$.

Team representatives meet for 3 minutes, then the teams meet for 5 minutes. At the animator's signal, the teams write their choices, then the two choices are announced.

k.   Round 10 is handled exactly as Round 9 was. Payoff points are squared.

l.   The entire group meets and the total for each team is announced.

---

* This exercise was originally called 'Prisoner's Dilemmas', from *Structured Experiences for Human Relations Training, Volume II,* by J.W. Pfeiffer and J.E. Jones, University Publishers, Inc., San Diego, pp. 52–54.

## Discussion questions

1. What did we learn from this game?
2. What increased the competitive spirit and what encouraged cooperation?
3. When did you feel most frustrated or angry, and why?
4. How is this related to real life? Give examples.
5. How is it possible to change a win–lose situation in life, into a win–win situation?

---

**Score sheet**

**Instructions:** For ten successive rounds, the Red team will choose either an 'A' or a 'B' and the Blue Team will choose either an 'X' or a 'Y'. The score each team receives in a round is determined by the pattern made by the choices of both teams, according to the schedule below.

**Scoring schedule**

AX — Both teams win 3 points

AY — Red Team loses 6 points; Blue Team wins 6 points.

BX — Red Team wins 6 points; Blue Team loses 6 points.

BY — Both teams lose 3 points.

| Round | Minutes | CHOICE | | CUMULATIVE POINTS | |
|---|---|---|---|---|---|
| | | Red Team | Blue Team | Red Team | Blue Team |
| 1 | 3 | | | | |
| 2 | 3 | | | | |
| 3 | 3 | | | | |
| 4* | 3 (reps) (teams) | | | | |
| 5 | 3 | | | | |
| 6 | 3 | | | | |
| 7 | 3 | | | | |
| 8 | 3 | | | | |
| 9 ** | 3 ( reps) 5 (teams) | | | | |
| 10 ** | 3 (reps) 5 (teams) | | | | |

\* Payoff points are doubled for this round only.

\*\* Payoff points are squared for these rounds (keep the minus sign).

## F.   Group reaction to the animator

The following is an excerpt from *Into the New Age* by Fr. Stephen Verney.

Groups often follow a long-term pattern which is expressed diagramatically like the one at the side here.

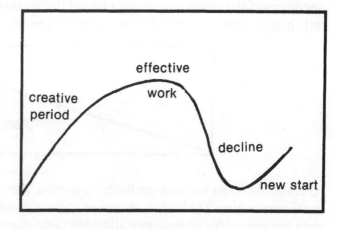

"There is a first phase when the group is enthusiastic and creative, and working out its purpose. This is followed by a second phase when it operates efficiently, and by a third phase during which it declines. When this third phase is reached, the group ought to be disbanded, or else should rethink and reformulate its purpose, and start again on a new upward creative phase . . .

"Within this long-term pattern, and often during a single meeting, groups may follow another pattern to which we have had cause to refer many times, the pattern of dependence–independence–interdependence. This is the normal development of every human life, as the child grows through adolescence and into responsible adulthood, but we find it re-enacted within a group situation, where it has to be lived through again and again. Each of us contains within oneself the child, the adolescent and the adult, and these elements in our personality can be activated by a situation which involves our relation to other people and to authority. Thus we find a group of adults, newly arrived at a conference where they do not know each other or the leader and staff, acting like children with an exaggerated dependence and obedience. After a while they are quite likely to challenge the platform, or to become worked up about some detail of administration in a way out of proportion to its importance. They may insist on some change in the programme, but once they have won a victory and made their mark and discovered that the leader is fallible, they will settle down to work together as responsible adults. In some mysterious way, the group has to relive this universal pattern of human development in order to grow itself.

"The leader must be aware of these processes, and must enable the groups to pass through them and so to develop and grow. This means that his/her style of leadership must be on a sliding scale which is illustrated in the diagram [on the next page].

> **But this self-knowledge is gained at a cost,**
> **and the cost is first of all to be borne by the leader.**

"At one end of the scale (s)he must be prepared to exercise an almost autocratic authority. The reason for this may be either that the group are feeling and behaving like children, and need to be told what to do, or that there is a crisis situation such as an outbreak of fire which allows no time to consult. As we move up the scale, we find the leader first explaining his/her decisions to the group, then asking for their opinions and discussing the question at issue, and finally leaving the decision in their hands. But the diagram shows that some modicum of authority has always to be retained, and some to be shared. Even in a battle when the military commander shouts to his troops "Charge!", he relies on their trust in himself, or at least their loyalty.

---

\* Stephen Verney, *Into the New Age*, Fount Publishers, William Collins Sons and Co., London, pp. 112–123.

"In moving from one style of leadership to another, as the group advances towards adulthood or regresses towards childhood, the leader may have to bear a lot of pain. The members of the group may project on to him/her their own fear and aggression, their guilt or self-hatred. They may attack him or her for something which they fear or dislike in

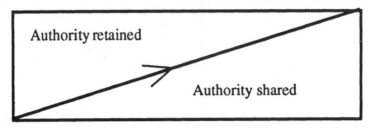

themselves – and because the leader is human, they are probably right in spotting this weakness in him. The leader, therefore, cannot simply sit back and think to him/herself, 'Now they are acting like adolescents attacking their parent, but of course the fault is in them not in me.' The leader must rather think, 'The fault is also in me but, because it is in them too, they notice it, and dislike it, and touch me in the soft spot, and I feel pain. But if I can expose myself to their attack, and if I can at the same time help them to understand why they are attacking me, then we can bring up into the light another area of human nature which we share together, and we can accept another weakness in ourselves and each other which can be transferred into a strength, or another point of injury which can become a point of healing.'

> **If healing is to take place, then it must also be borne by the members of the group.**

"So the cost must be borne by the leader, but if the healing process is going to take place, then it must also be borne by the members of the group. And here we come to the heart of the matter."

### The group as the place of forgiveness

"A.   The small group is an excellent place where a person comes to new self-awareness.

"This is generally a painful process, and it often happens suddenly and unexpectedly in the give and take of group life. We cannot go on pretending to one another and hiding what we really are, and as we get to know each other there comes perhaps a moment of irritation, perhaps a moment of deep friendship, when somebody lets slip a truth about ourselves. We are stabbed, as light penetrates into a dark place. Often what is revealed to us is something we knew on the intellectual level, but now we suddenly experience it at the emotional level. It hurts, because what is broken is some illusion about ourselves which we have cherished, and which seems to be the reason of our being and the mainspring of our activity. Suddenly we are made aware of the dark side of that very virtue on which we prided ourselves.

> **Elijah prayed that he might die, 'For I am no better than my fathers.'**

"Of course disillusion is in the end healthy, because to live under an illusion is both harmful to ourselves and destructive to others. But the moment of disillusion is dangerous, and is generally followed by depression, and can lead to the feeling that I am falling apart and losing control. At such a moment I need to be supported by the group, and particularly by the leader of the group – held together, as it were, so that I can let myself fall apart, and come face to face with a new area of my own ambivalence, and accept it, and find a new integration of myself round a new centre of truth. This is a kind of death and rebirth, a crisis in which the inter-locking of good and evil is transformed by death and resurrection.

"B.    Self-awareness goes hand in hand with awareness of others, and so it is that in the life of a small group we discover the depth and complexity of our relations with other people.

"An angry thought wounds, even though it is not expressed, and a caring thought builds up and supports. It is through the life of a small group that we come to know in our hearts what we have already accepted in our heads, that we and others are dependent on each other.

"Part of group life is tension, and the clash of personalities. You cannot avoid it. Every good group or team which is going to be creative, as indeed every good marriage, must experience the clash of personalities. This is so painful that many groups disband, and return to the simpler style of operating as individuals. But if they can face their own doubts – the betrayals which go hand and hand with their loyalty to each other – if they can dare to express their anger and despair to each other (not as accusations but in search for forgiveness), then they may be led through an experience of death and resurrection by which the good and evil within them may be unlocked. Then they may begin to discriminate, and to understand how the evil in one activates the evil in the other, but that at a deeper level there is a reality and a timeless present in which the true self of the one is united to the true self of the other.

"Out of such an experience of forgiveness, which may be on a little scale and often repeated, they can arrive at a new understanding of their interdependence. It is as though the bits of knowledge and insight which each one brought into the group has been fitted together like pieces of a puzzle, but there is a new quality of understanding as though all the bits have entered into each other like tongues of flame into a single fire. Now the group is entering together into the new age and what Paul prayed for is coming true:

> **'That you may understand with all the saints
> what is the breadth and length and height
> and depth of the love of Christ, and to know
> it, though it surpasses knowledge.'**

"C.    The third factor in this experience of forgiveness is coming to terms with authority and with the leadership of the group. This will be seen in an individual leader and at the same time be exercised by the group as a whole. Relationship to authority is one of the basic human problems, and it must be worked through (and at least partly resolved) by any person who is developing from the ego to the true self, as well as by any group who is developing towards the life of the new age. Authority is necessary if any creative advance is to be made – for example, an artist must have a frame within which he paints a picture.

"A new leader generally enjoys a honeymoon of goodwill, because people know instinctively that they need authority. Then inevitably, the leader becomes a problem because authority is a problem. From admiration her/his followers may change suddenly to scornful rejection. S/he was their ideal, their fantasy, their illusion of the perfect father or mother or godlike hero, and suddenly s/he is revealed to them in all his or her fallibility as a human being.

The group (be it large or small) gossips together over the fascinating topic of the leader's strengths and weaknesses, and begins to attack him or her publicly, but with apologies and protestations of loyalty. There is one school of thought which sees the whole behaviour of the group in terms of this situation where the group must react to authority, and there seems to be at least this truth in their theory, that authority is one strand which is plaited together with the other two (of self-knowledge and personal relations) to make the internal and on-going life of the group.

"The leader can react in a number of ways. S/he can focus the attention of the group upon its purpose, and thus relieve the pressure on himself or herself. The leader can make warm personal relationships with each individual member of the group, while retaining the command over the group as a whole. Both these tactics may be beneficial and promote the health of the group. But if the leader aspires to enable the group to live the life of the new age, then alongside and in conjunction with these two styles of leadership, the leader must adopt a third, which is to be one step ahead of the group in this very process of forgiveness which is its essence. That is to say, the leader must become more aware of the good and evil that interlock both in himself or herself and in the group, and the leader must pass through the experience of death and resurrection by which they may be unlocked and transformed. This the leader will have to do not once, but continuously.

> The leader (and the group)
> will have to pass
> through the experience of death
> and resurrection,
> not once, but continuously.

"These three areas of growth are present in every small group; whether it be a group of workers in industry, doctors and nurses in a clinic, or a village group. They are to grow in self-knowledge, awareness of others, and in the acceptance of a true authority. But they are realised more positively, and with less danger to those taking part, when the group is focused upon the presence of Christ, so that they may be experienced by each of the members and by the whole group as his way of forgiveness. The Christian Church has much to learn about group life, but it also has something to contribute, which is the story and the symbol of an unconditional forgiveness and the method of saying and acting it out within a company of people.

"It is in the small group that we are confronted by the total reality which is myself/the other/God, and where the different aspects of prayer take on a new quality. We can be silent together and come to know each other more profoundly than through words. We can utter needs, or our thanks, not in lengthy prayers but in a phrase, a monosyllable, somebody's name or need dropped into the silence, caught up in the flow of the river. We can study together, sharing not only our intellectual ideas, but our imaginative insights. Above all, we can act out the story and the symbol of forgiveness in its original simplicity."

> I have come
> that you may have life
> and have it
> to the full.
> **St. John 10: 10**

# Chapter 7

## Simple decision-making

## Action planning

**Included in this chapter:**

**A.** **Simple decision-making** .................................................................**95**

Decision-making exercise ............................................................95
Theory 1.  Involvement in decisions ............................................96
Theory 2.  Difficulties in decision-making ...................................98
Theory 3.  Making good decisions.................................................101
         4.  A simple guide for making decisions by
             consensus ......................................................................102
         5.  Who should make which decisions .....................................102
         6.  Factors which help decision-making .....................................103

**B.** **Action planning** ................................................................................**104**

         1.  Mapping the situation ........................................................104
         2.  7 Steps of Planning............................................................105
         3.  The 3 Cs ..........................................................................105
         4.  Force Field Analysis ..........................................................108
         5.  PERT.................................................................................109
         6.  Exercise on how to organise a workshop ...........................111
         7.  The planning kit ................................................................114

# Chapter 7

# Simple decision-making and action planning

## A. Simple decision-making

Every group has to make decisions, and the way in which these decisions are made will affect deeply the commitment of the members to the life and work of the group. If we have shared in the process of making a decision, we are far more likely to carry it out.

When a group cannot make decisions, the members become very frustrated. Most groups need some skill practice in decision-making so that all the members learn what helps and what hinders good decision-making.

### DECISION-MAKING EXERCISE

The following exercise can be used to give a group a common experience on which to reflect about their own patterns and problems in decision-making. After the discussion, the animator can add to the insights of the group by presenting whichever of the following theories seem most relevant to their needs.

### Procedure

a. Give the group an experience of making a real decision. This can be deciding about what to do with a free evening, or a reflection on real work in small groups (such as making codes). Or the animator can arrange a fishbowl exercise giving those in the middle responsibility to make a decision.

b. After the group has made the decision, the animator asks the group to identify what major problems they had in reaching the decision. The animators then decide which theory is most relevant.

c. The appropriate theory is given as a short lecture. Handouts are given to each participant on this theory.

d. The animator then asks the group either to form groups of 3 or go back to their work groups. In small groups they discuss which of the problems of decision-making they experienced.

e. Bring the whole group back together and discuss the problems of decision-making.

f. After discussing these problems, ask the group what they can do as a group to improve their decision-making. In this way, they will set their own norms and guidelines and be more likely to abide by them.

### Theory 1: INVOLVEMENT IN DECISIONS*

The more concerned we are that a community take an active role in carrying out a decision, the more important it is that they share as fully as possible in making the decision.

If we look back on how many people were actively involved in making a decision, we will find they all fall somewhere along this line:

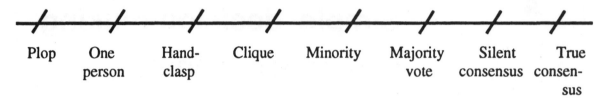

| Plop | One person | Hand-clasp | Clique | Minority | Majority vote | Silent consensus | True consensus |

### The plop

Here the group makes a decision by **not** making a decision. 'Not to decide — is to decide.' Someone makes a suggestion, but it drops like a stone into a pond, and no one pays any attention to it at all. If the person who made the suggestion really felt enthusiastic about it, the fact that it was totally ignored could make that person withdraw or resist later suggestions.

### The one-person decision

This is quickly made, but later when the decider depends on free or voluntary support from others to implement it (s)he may find himself/herself carrying it out alone.

**Topic jumping.** One person can also prevent a group reaching a decision by introducing a new point just as the group is ready to decide something. If the point is relevant it should be allowed, though it should have been brought in earlier. If it is not relevant it should be recognised as a distraction or an attempt by one person to control the group, and should not be allowed to prevent the group from making a decision.

### The handclasp

One person makes a suggestion. Another says, "What a marvellous idea," and without further discussion, the matter is decided. These decisions are more frequent than one thinks, and often pass unnoticed at the time, but resentment comes to the surface later.

---

* Adapted from the *Basic Reader in Human Relations Training*, Episcopal Church, Part I, pp. 84–89.

## The clique

This decision is made by a small group who plan beforehand to get their way. Because they are better organised than those who disagree, they are often successful on the immediate issue, but they bring a spirit of rivalry rather than co-operation into the group. Sometimes groups of people who have formerly been excluded or silent **form a caucus** in order to present a common agenda. This can be a very positive action and check-and-balance to a dominant group. It is a healthy sign in a participatory democracy.

## Minority

These decisions are not as consciously organised as those of the clique, but a few powerful personalities dominate the group, often unconsciously, and then later they wonder why the others are apathetic.

## Majority vote

In big groups this is often the most effective way to make a decision. However, one may lose the interest or the loyalty of the minority who voted against a decision, especially if they feel their point of view was not heard.

## Silent consensus

Some groups aim at unanimous decisions. These are good, if genuine, but they are rarely achieved completely on important issues. Unanimous agreement is sometimes assumed, when some members have not felt free to disagree and have kept silent.

## Consensus

This is an agreement, often involving compromise or the combination of various possibilities, after all opinions have been heard. Disagreements and minority viewpoint are discussed fully. It takes time and care to build a climate in which all feel free to express themselves, but this method does build unity, cooperation and commitment. It does not mean listening to people and then doing what we were going to do in the first place. It means adapting to accommodate the concerns of all. It may take longer to make a decision this way, but it will often be carried out more quickly and wholeheartedly.

---

### Who should make which decisions?

It is neither possible nor desirable to involve everybody in every decision. One of the main skills of democratic leadership is deciding who should be involved in making which decisions. The basic rule is that the more deeply people are affected by a decision, the more important it is they should share in making it.

---

### Theory 2: DIFFICULTIES IN DECISION-MAKING *

Every group, to achieve its goal, is constantly involved in making decisions:
- big decisions
- little decisions
- easy decisions
- hard decisions
- right decisions
- wrong decisions

but always decisions, decisions, decisions.

Decision-making forms a continuing pattern of relationships among members of a group: a pattern in which every individual member has some influence. It is amazing the effect a bit of information here, a loud objection there, an expression of approval or hostility, envy or admiration, contempt or condescension, can have on an impending decision.

So it is little wonder that group after group has difficulty making decisions. Some become paralysed when confronted with a decision; some argue over a minor point; others rush into a vote only to reverse their decision later on or fail to carry out the plan; others appoint a committee (or look for a saviour) to save them from having to decide.

Most of the difficulties encountered by a group in making decisions centre around one or another of the following factors:

### a. Fear of consequences

In some groups the possible outcomes of an impending decision may bring divisions and disagreements. Frank acknowledgement of these fears often suggests how they can be dealt with effectively, e.g. "If my boss knows I am in this group challenging corruption, will I lose my job?"

### b. Conflicting loyalties

When one person is a member of a number of groups, this frequently leads to divided loyalties about decisions. An atmosphere in which it is possible for these conflicts to be brought out into the open without threat to the individual is a great help in resolving them. (E.g. "I'd like to help with this community project, but I hardly get any time to spend with my wife and children these days.")

---

\* Adapted from the *Basic Reader in Human Relations Training,* Part I, pp.84–89.

### c.   Interpersonal conflict

In groups of any size personal differences occur which provoke feelings of affection or dislike among members and which interfere with sound decision-making. Power struggles when two different people are each trying to get their way are common. Often another member who is not involved in the interpersonal conflict can bring the real problem into the open.

### d.   Hidden agenda

One person may try to get the group to make a certain decision, which (s)he wants for reasons which he or she will not share with the group.

### e.   Blundering methods

A group may be so bound by rigid procedures (e.g. always addressing all remarks to the chairperson) that there is little chance for free expression of differences. **Or** a group may allow itself to substitute personal opinion for adequate information. **Or** a group may approach the decision-making process without testing for consensus.

### f.   Inadequate leadership

A leader may hinder good decision-making if (s)he restricts the expression of opinion or discussion on issues too soon. Leaders also may fail to provide assistance in selecting appropriate methods for decision-making or be insensitive to the factors causing difficulty in the group.

### g.   Clash of interests

Sometimes different groups or individuals within an organisation do have opposing interests (e.g. workers wanting higher wages and owners wanting higher profits). This type of conflict, involving issues of justice, will be dealt with more fully in Chapter 9.

## Moving towards the goal

As a group moves towards its goal, it seldom proceeds in a straight course from 'A' to 'B':

A _____ B

Rather its movement is usually up and down and around, sometimes even ending up at 'C' instead of its original goal of 'B'. Sometimes this unexpected decision may be better than the one that was expected.

**Theory 3:    MAKING GOOD DECISIONS \***

This theory can be explained and used as a tool for midway evaluation when a group is working together on a project.

In making any major decision, some problems must be solved along the way, each of which involves a number of smaller decisions. One can identify six basic needs in the movement of a group towards its goal. Of course no group moves directly through the six problem areas in a given order. There is constant movement back and forth among them; but they are always present in various ways at various times requiring various decisions.

**a.    Need:   information**

What is our situation? Who are we? Where are we? What is our common ground? What are the limits within which we must work? Who or what brought us together? Until a group recognises its actual present situation, by gathering the information about that situation, any attempt to suggest goals is premature.

**b.    Need:   the goal**

Where do we want to go? What do we want to do? What choices are open to us? Until there is general agreement on the goal, the group will not move effectively. Members of a group who have not accepted the goal or who have had little choice in choosing it, tend to be unco-operative. The setting of a goal is usually tentative at first, and must be re-examined from time to time in order to test if it is suitable.

**c.    Need:   freedom of the people involved**

How free are we to move? If a group is to be creative, individuals must be free to act, to offer insights, to test ideals, to make contributions, to share the leadership without fear. Such functions as encouraging, harmonising, and supporting are needed to maintain an atmosphere of freedom. Sometimes outside factors which limit the free participation of group members need to be discussed openly.

---

\*  Adapted from the *Basic Reader in Human Relations Training*, Part I, pp. 84– 89.

### d. Need: the plan

How do we get there? How do we achieve our goal? What procedures do we need? What resources do we need? As a group finds the best ways and means, routes and methods, necessary to get started, members become more and more involved in initiating, clarifying, summarising, and testing for consensus.

### e. Need: check on progress

Where are we now? Where are we in the process of settling all the other problems? Are we going in the right direction? How far have we got? Do we know where we are? Do we need to change our goal or our procedures? Is everyone still with us?

From time to time a group must stop, make a progress report to itself. Many a group has failed to reach its goal because it assumed everyone knew what was happening in the group when, actually, confusion reigned.

### f. Need: outcome

Where have we arrived? Have we reached our goal? What have we decided or achieved? It may not be the original goal, but is it satisfactory?

## 4. A SIMPLE GUIDE FOR MAKING DECISIONS BY CONSENSUS *

a. What are we trying to decide? (Be sure this is clear to everyone.)
b. What are the different possibilities? (Consider as many as possible. Brainstorming may be useful.)
c. How may each possibility work? Pros and cons.
d. What suggestion, or combination of suggestions, do we choose?
f. Who will do what,
      when,
      where, and
      how?

## 5. WHO SHOULD MAKE WHICH DECISIONS?

If all decisions are made by a group, a great deal of time may be wasted on unimportant matters. There are many situations where it is sensible to delegate the power to make decisions to one person or a small group, e.g. details of carrying out a policy which the whole group has agreed to.

However, the more important the consequences of a decision, the more important it is to involve the people concerned in the decision.

Group involvement is particularly important when:
a. various points of view and opinions are needed
b. when the group is directly affected by the decision (the project affects them, or money is involved)
c. when the group must carry out the decision
d. when the group has learnt to work effectively together, sharing leadership functions, and handling decision-making procedures easily

---

* From Nancy Geyer and Shirley Noll, *Team Building in Church Groups* (Judson Press: Valley Forge, Pa.), 1970.

## 6.  FACTORS WHICH HELP DECISION-MAKING *

a.  Clear goal.

b.  Clear understanding of who has responsibility for the decision.

c.  Good means of stimulating and sharing ideals (e.g. a code, film or diagram).

d.  Effective leadership and structures to deal with the size of the group.

e.  Effective way of testing different suggestions offered.

f.  Commitment of the leader to genuine group involvement in making the decision.

g.  Agreement beforehand on what procedures will be most appropriate (e.g. consensus, majority vote, secret ballot, etc.).

---

### Clear goals are vital

Unity, commitment, and energy grow strikingly in a group when there is a clear goal which all believe in.

---

### Actions must take place

"The Assemblies must dedicate themselves to solving concrete problems in the people's lives, making every effort to resolve them. Difficulties in water supply to a communal village or suburb, difficulties in outlets for goods produced by the people, the school that must be opened, the road that must be cut in the middle of the bush, the shop that must be opened, the cooperative that must be supported, the cultural and sporting activities that are disorganised – these are some of the problems that should preoccupy our Assemblies, that each deputy must study and resolve in the people's interest. The Assemblies must guarantee that all citizens get effective support and a non-bureaucratic solution to their problems within existing possibilities, from the state services. The Assemblies must punish severely those civil servants who by their behaviour, reveal neglect, incompetence or insensitivity towards the people."

*Samora Machel Speaks,* Black Liberation Press, Box 955, NY, NY 10027, p. 19.

---

* Adapted from the *Basic Readers in Human Relations Training,* Part I, pp. 84-89

## B.  Action planning

The following exercise can help a group that has reached the stage of planning action. Further guidelines on setting goals will be found in Chapter 10.

### 1.  MAPPING YOUR NETWORK

This exercise deals with the first need described in Theory 2 (page 98) – Decision-making:  information about the situation.

**Procedure**

a.  Divide the group into teams that work together in real situations.

b.  Ask each team to draw on a piece of newsprint a "map" of their situation. This includes every group, organisation and category of people in their environment that they relate to, try to influence, work with, etc. They should draw their own team in the picture.

c.  When they have finished, ask them to answer the following questions:
   i.  Which of these groups or units are you really trying to influence?
   ii.  How well are you doing this?
   iii.  Look critically at each of these groups in relation to their class position (see Chapter 9 for a deeper explanation).
   iv.  How good is the relation with each unit?
   v.  In what areas do you have a problem?
   vi.  How can you improve it?

d.  One way to share this information between teams is to ask each team to put their "map" on the wall and have participants walk around looking at them. Anyone with questions can ask them after they have seen all the maps.

**Time**   Between 1 and 2 hours, depending on the complexity of the situation being looked at.

**Materials**  Crayons and newsprint for each team. Tape.

---

**Very often when a divided group complains of poor communication, the root of the problem is that there is an unspoken disagreement on goals.**

---

> **2. SEVEN STEPS OF PLANNING ***
>
> This outline helps a real working group plan practically.
> a. Diagnosis.
>    What are the problems?
>    What are the needs?
> b. What do we want to achieve (objective) in a particular period?
>    This week, this month, this year?
> c. What are the possible ways of achieving this objective?
>    Brainstorm for proposals.
> d. What are the advantages and disadvantages of each proposal?
>    How much time, money and personal effort will be needed for each proposal?
> e. Which proposal (plan) do we accept?
>    This may include several suggestions.
> f. **Who** will do **what, when, where** and **how?**
> g. At what point do we need to evaluate?
>    Who should be involved in the evaluation?

Note: Force Field Analysis can be one way to work through steps b, c, and d of the 7 steps above.

## 3. THE 3 Cs – COOPERATION, CAMPAIGN, CONFRONTATION

This model is extremely useful when a practical goal has been decided upon, more support is needed, and it becomes clear that certain people or groups are blocking the achievement of this goal. It is also helpful when there is debate about different approaches to change (for example, if some people think that only one type of action can be useful when in fact many different approaches are needed). This analysis can help unite people using different tactics to achieve a common goal.

When an individual or a small group of poor and powerless people make a request, they are often totally ignored. It is as if a mouse were squeaking at a lion. Those in control stand on a solid platform of power. (See "different types of power" in Chapter 10.)

> **When spider webs unite,
> they can tie up a lion**
> – Ethiopia

Very often the only power which the poor have is that of their numbers. But numbers of people are not powerful unless they are united and organised.

---
* Adapted from handouts given at the Christian Education Leadership Training program, South Africa.

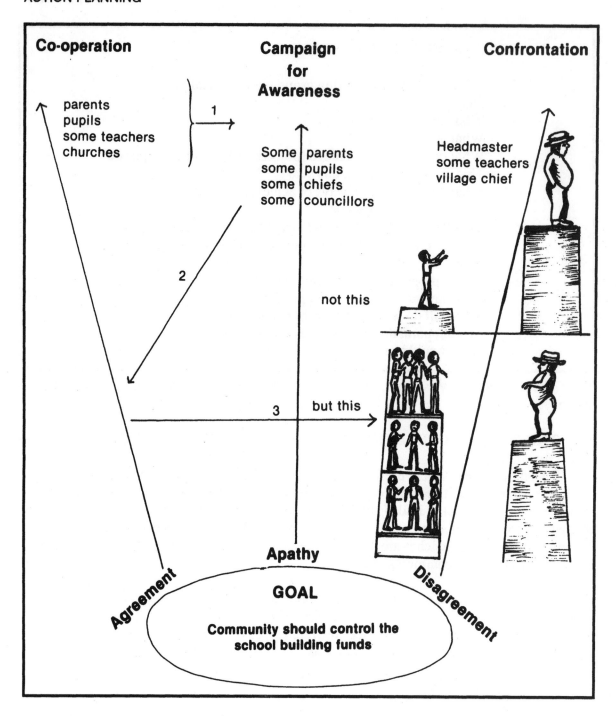

**Procedure**

a. The first step is to list, on the left, all the individuals and groups who agree on the importance of the goal. Plan how to get these actively involved in a **process of cooperation.**

b. List, in the middle, the names of individuals and groups which are at present apathetic and passive, but which would have much to gain if the goal was achieved. Plan a **campaign for awareness** for these people and groups, cooperating with those who already agree on the need for change. The campaign aims to draw those who are at present apathetic across to the side of those who agree and cooperate. (Codes can be very useful in this campaign.)

c. List, on the right, the names of those who disagree with the change, paying particular attention to people or groups that are in a position to block the change and prevent the group reaching its goal.

**It will be necessary** to **challenge** or confront these groups and individuals. The first challenge may be in the form of a dialogue. If this does not succeed, those working for the change may have to consider some form of confrontation or pressure.

Confrontation can take the form of withholding money or labour. "We will not contribute any more money until . . ." or "We will strike on Monday unless . . ." It can also make use of publicity, newspaper articles, etc., and seek to arouse public opinion.

If all of these fail, some groups eventually turn to armed struggle. If the original goal is a reasonable and just one, and all the other means have been tried, it is those who resist the change who are responsible for the use of violence. The degree of violence used in any struggle for change is usually in direct proportion to the degree of violence used by those in power to prevent the change from happening.

**Time**      2 – 3 hours.

**Materials**   Newsprint, felt pens, tape.

---

Freedom doesn't come like a bird on a wing,
doesn't come down like the summer's rain,
Freedom, Freedom is a hard-won thing,
You've got to work for it,
Fight for it,
Day and night for it,
And every generation's got to do it again.

– Old trade union song

---

107

## 4.   FORCE FIELD ANALYSIS *

This model should be used with groups that have already analysed their situation and decided on a major goal. Often this goal is very ambitious and not immediately attainable. Force Field Analysis can help them to find useful intermediate goals which will help move the situation towards the major goal.

It is helpful to look at the forces which are helping us reach the goal, and those which are hindering (or pushing in the opposite direction).

### Procedure

a.   It is best to work with this model in groups of 3 – 5 people who share a common goal and work in the same situation.

b.   Ask the group to draw the following diagram on newsprint, defining briefly **the present situation** and the **major goal.** They should write one summary statement about each of these along the vertical lines.

c.   Then ask the group to list the helping forces on the left side, drawing longer or shorter arrows to indicate the strength of the forces which are pushing the present situation towards the goal.

   On the right-hand side, list the hindering forces which prevent change or reduce its power. Again use longer or shorter arrows to indicate the strength of these forces.

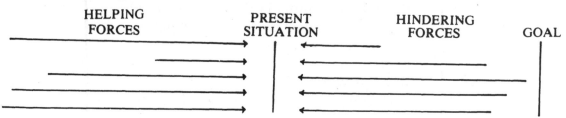

| HELPING FORCES | PRESENT SITUATION | HINDERING FORCES | GOAL |

d.   Explain that one can move towards the goal
   **either** by increasing the helping forces,
   **or** by weakening the hindering forces.
   Sometimes the more pressure that comes from the helping forces, the more resistance develops in the hindering forces. In such cases, it is often best to start by reducing the hindering forces.

e.   Now ask the group to choose
   **either** one of the helping forces which they could strengthen,
   **or** one of the hindering forces which they could reduce or weaken.
   Taking this "force" as the new situation, ask them to identify their goal in regard to working with this force.

f.   Once again, draw a new diagram listing the helping and hindering forces related to this new sub-goal. This process can be done 2 or 3 times.

### Summary

The work on the diagrams stimulates a process of intense communication in the group and helps them to work out a strategy involving one or more clear sub-goals, which will be concrete steps towards the major goal.

**Time**      2 or more hours.

**Materials**  Newsprint, markers and tape.

---

* Saul Eisen, *A Problem Solving Program*, NTL, Washington, D.C, 1201 16th Street, N.W. 20036.

## 5.    PERT:    PROGRAM EVALUATION AND REVIEW TECHNIQUE *

After a group has decided on its goal, it is essential to organise activities to achieve the goal. For local groups, it is easier to use the Planning Kit explained in the next exercise. For larger programs, it can be very helpful to do a PERT, using it as **a visual chart.**

This can be important to a team because:
- it shows how simple or complex the plan is
- it leads to realistic planning
- it organises activities in a way that ensures the goal can be reached
- it helps motivate and keeps the team to deadlines
- it provides immediate information for self-evaluation

### How to do a PERT

Events are usually the end of the task and do not take much time in themselves. Let us use an example of hiring a new literacy coordinator. The following tasks will have to be done:

1.    decision to hire a new literacy coordinator
2.    a selection committee to be formed
3.    a job description developed
4.    recruitment of candidates  to begin
5.    candidates to be interviewed
6.    final selection to be made.

In this example, one can see that one activity **must** follow the other.

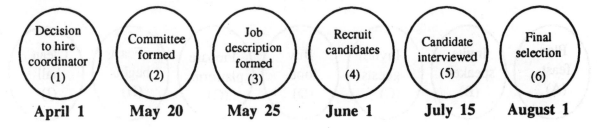

| Decision to hire coordinator (1) | Committee formed (2) | Job description formed (3) | Recruit candidates (4) | Candidate interviewed (5) | Final selection (6) |
|---|---|---|---|---|---|
| **April 1** | **May 20** | **May 25** | **June 1** | **July 15** | **August 1** |

If the group  has a deadline, it is important **to plan time backwards.** For example, if you want to have the final selection of the candidate made by August 1, all of the candidates might have to be interviewed before July 15, etc.

1 ←———— 2 ←———— 3 ←———— 4 ←———— 5 ←———— 6
April 1        May 20        May 25        June 1        July 15        August 1

---

\*    Adapted from the MDI Group, *Leadership: The Responsible Exercise of Power*, Cincinnati, Ohio, p. H-6.

However, sometimes tasks can be done at the same time and they do not have to follow one another in order. For example, if you were organising a feast these might be some of the tasks:

A. plan the feast
B. invite the guest speaker
C. invite the guests
D. buy the food
E. decorate the hall
F. cook the food
G. prepare the platform
H. feast begins
I. clean the hall

**June 1**                                                              **December 1**

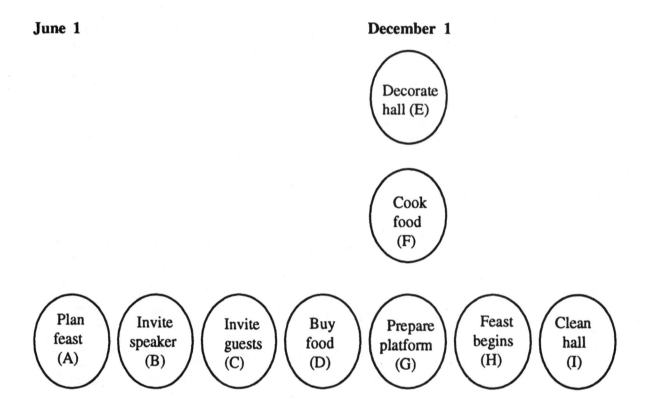

In this example it is easy to see that E, F, and G (decorate the hall, cook the food and prepare the platform) will all have to happen at the same time. On the other hand, the amount of time needed before the feast would depend on how many people are to be involved and the availability of the guest speaker. If the group hopes to have a "famous" person, like a Cabinet Minister, to be the guest speaker, they may well have to plan the event six months in advance. If the guest speaker is a local chief, it might be possible to plan the feast only one month in advance.

PERT is a commonsense tool which helps remind people of the preparation work needed before an event, and check if the tasks are being completed on schedule.

## 6.   EXERCISE ON HOW TO ORGANISE A WORKSHOP

The following exercise is helpful in training people who will be responsible for planning workshops on a district level.

**Procedure**

a.   The following form on "organising a workshop" is given to all participants. Each person is asked to complete the form by doing two tasks:

   i.   placing the tasks in order by numbering the task according to what will come first; put a number "1", second a number "2", third a number "3" and so forth.
   ii.   make a timetable of events on a separate piece of paper.

b.   The animator can give an arbitrary date for the workshop, such as May 1 – 5. S/he also shows how to do a PERT timetable using the illustrations given above.

c.   After each individual has completed the above tasks, ask participants to form small groups to compare their diagrams. Each small group can then make one diagram on a piece of newsprint.

d.   These diagrams can be put on the walls for each small group to compare their own. The animator can choose one or two groups' diagrams which include the major points most clearly, or ask a small group to share their PERT.

**Organising a workshop**
**(Participant's work form)**

You are a member of a core team responsible for helping give workshops for parishes and the district. You are responsible for planning, administering and staffing the workshop. Below you will find a list of 17 items that need to be done to make sure the workshop will take place.

**Place in order** the following tasks according to what you think needs to be done first, second, etc. Put a number "1", a number "2", a number "3", etc. in the space provided.

Example:      13   A
              3    B
              6    C

Those tasks you think need to be done at the same time can be given the same number. When you have finished putting these tasks in order with numbers on the form or a separate piece of paper, arrange the letters (tasks) in the order needed according to a timetable. For this exercise, assume the workshop will be held on May 1 – 5.

———————A.   Hold the planning meeting of all the staff for workshop, going into the details of who will do what in each session.

———————B.   Send the letters of invitation to participants, including a questionnaire asking them their expectations.

———————C.   Make booking for conference centre and pay deposit.

———————D.   Evaluate, with the staff, details and changes they would have made in the whole workshop.

E.   Pick up films.

———————F.   Core team meets with the local group to plan the purpose of the workshop, dates, venues, and who participants will be.

G.   Pay conference centre and other invoices.

———————H.   Workshop begins.

———————I.   Core team meets to clarify the purpose of the workshop, selects appropriate staff, outlines initial plan and all materials needed for the workshop.

J.   Materials are collected to take to the workshop.

K.   Reminders are sent to all staff about the dates of the workshop and the time of the planning meeting of staff. This also includes a map to the conference centre.

L.   Return films.

M.   Reminders about time and place are sent to all participants who are invited to come to the workshop. Include a map.

———————N.   Book films.

———————O.   Reconfirm booking at the conference centre, giving exact number of people expected.

———————P.   Duplicate handouts needed for the workshop.

———————Q.   Send letters of invitation to the staff needed.

## EXAMPLE OF A PERT FOR ORGANISING A WORKSHOP

The following example of a PERT is one way to plan a workshop; however, participants may develop a better plan. The animator should have this example written on newsprint and be prepared to share this example with the whole group or the results of some of the other small groups which are similar to this example. S/he asks the groups to compare this plan with their own plan, noting carefully the differences and deciding which plan is more realistic for their own situation.

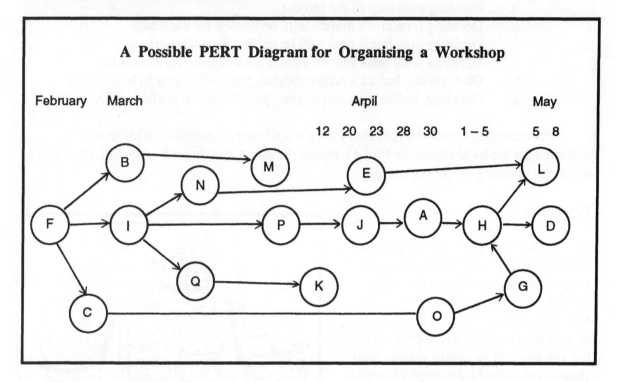

**A Possible PERT Diagram for Organising a Workshop**

**Time**      About 2 hours

**Materials**   Newsprint, markers, tape, a copy of "organising a workshop" form and one clean sheet of paper for each participant.

## 7. THE PLANNING KIT

The idea of using a series of pictures to help groups plan a project comes from the Village Education Resources Centre in Bangladesh. The purpose of using visual methods for planning is to help people **see** what is needed to start and complete a practical project.

The planning process includes the following steps:

- a. Choosing a specific project
- b. Planning each step of the project
- c. Deciding how much money will be needed for each step
- d. Deciding how much time will be needed for each step
- e. Deciding what other resources will be necessary for the project
- f. Discovering, before a project begins, the profit likely to be realised
- g. Deciding, before a project begins, how the group profits will be used

For example, a group has decided to begin a sewing cooperative to make school uniforms for the local school, or start a cooperative union garden on 5 acres of land. At this point, the planning kit is very useful.

### Procedure

Before the meeting, the animator (with the help of 1 or 2 people experienced in marketing, dress-making, agriculture, etc.) should list all the steps they can think of which will be necessary in the project. They should make (or ask an artist to make) simple clear sketches of each of these steps, on separate sheets of paper, about 8 inches by 4 inches. There should be several additional sheets of paper ready for quick sketches, symbols or key words, showing steps which the group may mention that they have not thought of.

The animator should also have plenty of slips of paper marked clearly: $5, $10, $100. If possible, use the colour of the paper of the real bank notes of your country.

## Step 1:     Order of work

a.     The animator asks the group to discuss in 2s and 3s all the steps they will need to take, to start and complete their sewing project. Once they have been actively involved in this process, bring the group together and ask them to sit in a semicircle facing a wide empty wall.

b.     Ask them what they will have to do first. Find the picture of the first thing they suggest and put it up on the wall near to the left. Ask if everyone agrees that this is the first step.

     If something is suggested that comes before this step, move the first picture a little to the right and put the second on the left-hand side of the first suggestion.

     Together the group builds up the line of pictures, showing each step that needs to be taken, in **the correct order, on the wall.**

c.     If something is suggested for which there is no picture, the animator quickly draws a picture or a symbol.

d.     If there are pictures left over showing steps that noone has mentioned, the animator shows these to the group, and they discuss whether these steps are really necessary in their project. If so, they put them in the correct place, moving other pictures along to the right.

### Step 2: Time for work

a. The animator asks them to discuss in 2s or 3s how long each step will take, (S)he then puts the number of weeks or months on the wall under each picture.

b. If there is a deadline for one part of the activity (e.g. first day of school year if they are making uniforms, or the time of rains for planting if it is an agricultural project), starting from this date and **moving backwards** and forwards, the group works out when each step must be started and finished.

Together they see clearly when they must start, when they can expect to finish, and what they expect to accomplish each week.

### Step 3: Money for work

a. The animator gives the group another opportunity to buzz in small groups on how much money will be needed for each step.

b. Once again, the whole group goes systematically through each step and puts the amount of money needed beneath each picture.

c. They add up how much money they need in total.

d. They work out how much they will probably produce and how much they will make as a group.

### Step 4: Help for work

Once again, the group goes through each step discussing whether they will need help, from a resource person, or from other members of the community (e.g. a seamstress, nurse, agricultural expert, etc.). These can be put up on the place where the person will be needed.

### Step 5: Use of profit

a. As this is a communal project, it is important for the group to decide, before the project starts, how the money will be used once the project is complete. If this is not done now, there may be serious disagreements at the end of the project.

b.    The animator can prepare a further series of pictures for an illiterate group, or use words for a literate group, of all the possible ways in which money may be used.

This would include:
- paying back any loans
- dividing profits equally amongst group members
- buying new tools or equipment
- starting new projects (e.g. poultry, vegetable gardens, day-care centre, literacy class)
- getting water pipes
- building a community school, etc.

This is a good opportunity to stimulate the imagination of the group about the different alternatives and to help them imagine how they could improve their lives in the future. It helps them to realise that development is an ongoing process not limited to one project.

c.    The animator puts up one by one the pictures of possible ways of spending the money, giving the members an opportunity to explain each one as it goes up. Then in small groups of 4 or 5, they are asked to make recommendations as to how the money will be spent. When they have done this, each group chooses a representative to send to a group in the middle. This group shares the recommendations of each group, and discusses them until they reach an agreement on how much should be spent on what. This agreement should be written down. If the pictures and dates and money cannot be kept on the wall, these should be written on a large calendar, and the group can check regularly to see if they are completing each step in time.

**This planning kit is only helpful to a group which has already discussed its needs thoroughly and is ready to decide on a practical project.**

# Chapter 8

## Evaluation

**This chapter includes:**

**A. Preparatory workshop for participatory evaluation** ................................. 122

1. What is evaluation ................................................................. 122
2. Evaluation exercise ............................................................... 123
3. Why do we evaluate? ............................................................. 123
4. Problems exercise ................................................................. 124
5. When do we evaluate? ........................................................... 125
6. Ethics of evaluation .............................................................. 125
7. Planning questions and indicators for specific programs ................. 125
8. Methods of evaluation ........................................................... 126
9. Historical reflection with slides, photos or drawings ..................... 127
10. Planning the program for participatory evaluation ......................... 130

**B. Evaluation exercises for workshop** .............................................. 131

1. Simple and reliable ............................................................... 131
2. One word or feelings ............................................................. 131
3. Listing the main parts of the program ....................................... 132
4. Why do we do what we do? ..................................................... 132

# Chapter 8
# Evaluation

**The only way forward
is to take one step back.**

Most development workers are so totally involved with the day-to-day activities of programs that it is very difficult to see what are the overall weaknesses and strengths. The result is that projects are soon run on a perpetual crisis basis. Planning is forgotten, co-ordination is non-existent and resources are not used properly. How often have people from the same development office gone to work in the same area, and not coordinated their efforts?

Evaluation needs to be a constant process built into all levels of a program:
      a.    by the participants in all projects
      b.    by animators
      c.    by development coordinators and administrators

Evaluation also needs to be done:
      a.    at the end of learning events,
      b.    at key points in a group (literacy classes, women's clubs, agricultural projects) at least once a month,
      c.    at regular times in a project (e.g. at the end of each year before planning the next year's program).

The value of evaluation includes:
- seeing our success,
- assessing our weaknesses,
- clarifying what needs to be changed or strengthened.

There are two major exercises on evaluation presented in this chapter.

- Participatory evaluation of projects and programs
- Evaluation exercise for work-shops.

# A. Preparatory workshop for participatory evaluation

Participatory evaluation is a process of involving participants in programs to reflect critically on their own projects, programs, aims and leadership. **It is participant-centred.** It is an important part of the development education process. Its value is that it continues the process of action-reflection, and increases the awareness that people themselves can shape their own lives and destiny.

The steps involved come from a workshop model introduced by Daudi Nturibi of World Education.*

These steps include:
- What is evaluation?
- Problems about evaluation
- Why do we evaluate?
- When do we evaluate?
- Ethics of evaluation
- Planning questions and indicators of evaluation
- Methods of evaluation
- Planning the program for evaluation.

The following exercises and guided discussions are the basis of developing the skills for beginning the participatory evaluation process. This model can be used in its entirety (which would take from 3 – 4 days) or parts of it can be used.

## 1. WHAT IS EVALUATION?

This is a quick brainstorming session. The question posed to the group is, "What do you think evaluation means?" These answers are put on newsprint after the group has discussed them in small groups first.

At this point it is useful for the animator to give a short input on what participatory evaluation is. Participatory evaluation requires the participants of a program or a project to take an active part in its evaluation. The people themselves examine the strengths and the weaknesses so that they can contribute more to the success of their own work. All the information shared by the participants during this kind of evaluation is for their own benefit and is made available to them. Its main purpose is to have a positive effect on their own lives and the community of which they are a part.

This type of evaluation is very different from the usual evaluation by an outside expert, often employed by a funding agency. Their main purpose is to check whether the funds are being well used, and often it is just a fact-finding, but not an educational, process. The criterion of what "well used" means is decided by outsiders and not by those carrying out the program or the participants in the program.

---

* James McAffery and Noreen Clark, *Demystifying Evaluation*, World Education, New York, 1978.

## 2. EVALUATION EXERCISE:  A non-threatening trial run

a.   Four topics are chosen, written on sheets of paper and placed on the walls as far apart as possible. Participants are asked to select one of these topics.  They sit under the following headings and  evaluate the topics as  fully as possible by writing down evaluation statements on newsprint. The four  topics could be:

   i.   An introductory exercise all have used earlier.

   ii.   The breakfast or meal they have just eaten.

   iii.   The conference centre they are using.

   iv.   Transport in the country.

Each group has about 10 –15 minutes to note down evaluation statements on the topic.

When this task is completed, each group goes around the room and looks at the other evaluation statements.

b.   The groups are asked to move clockwise to a different topic; for example, the group that wrote evaluation statements on transport might move to the breakfast statements. The new group now needs to study each statement carefully, and then write a question that was being answered by each of the statements made previously. They are also asked to write other questions that could have been in the minds of the original group.

The purpose of this exercise is to recognise that, behind every evaluatory statement, we all have assumptions, values, and questions. There is a standard, an expectation, or a set of values that we consciously or unconsciously are trying to reach. It is therefore important for people who are doing evaluation to be clear about the assumptions, values and standards which they are setting for themselves.

c.   When this task is completed, the whole group goes to each of the topics and the questions are read to the whole group. In this way they all consider the questions related to all four topics.

d.   If there is time, one could ask the group what they feel they have learnt from the exercise.

## 3. WHY DO WE EVALUATE?

Through a brainstorming exercise, the whole group gives suggestions explaining in general why we evaluate ourselves, our programs and our projects. These are listed on newsprint. This is a short exercise.

## 4.  PROBLEMS ABOUT EVALUATION

a.  Ask participants to write down their main problems, worries, or concerns about the process of evaluating a program, project or group. List these problems on newsprint. Encourage them to include their worries about the participatory evaluation method. This session takes some time and should not be rushed. A lot of information comes from it and the group's feeling about the whole evaluation will be affected by it.

Point out at the end of this session that evaluation where people are involved needs very careful attention. The work that needs to be done must be thought through carefully to make it meaningful, clear and simple for others. An outside evaluation which does not involve the participants can be done very easily, but its results are quite different.

b.  From the long list of problems involved in evaluation, the next step is to classify the areas which these problems deal with. Participants are asked to read slowly through all the points put on newsprint in the previous session, and to suggest key areas. This discussion can take a long time, but the exercise is useful to help people in classifying ideas.

However, if the workshop is short and the participants have little experi ence in evaluation, the animators and planning team can take the first list and categorise the problems for the group. This depends on the aim of the workshop. Do you want the participants to concentrate on evaluating their work, or do you want them to learn skills of evaluation?

**Summary**

The following headings could be useful as a checklist to see if the participants have covered all areas. All questions need to be included under one of these headings:

**We need to evaluate**
- aims
- ethics
- participation
- methods
- content:  expectations, materials, language and touchy issues
- animators
- follow-up
- venues
- time and money
- planning, coordination, administration
- decision-making.

Not all these areas need to be evaluated at the same time, but at some time they do.

## 5.  WHEN DO WE EVALUATE?

In small groups, the question is asked, "When do we evaluate?" The whole group discussion on this point can be very helpful, for it clarifies whether the evaluation is meant for outsiders or for the people themselves. Ideally, participants should be self-reliant and carry out their own evaluation as they sense the need arises. However, this often does not happen, either because of time or because of conflicts in a group.

Therefore groups need to be encouraged to have regular evaluations to avoid the problem of evaluating too late (when a crisis has become too big) or too early (when there is not much to evaluate).

## 6.  ETHICS OF EVALUATION

As an introduction to this session, it is useful to clarify again what we mean by evaluation where people are involved. Some large research and evaluation projects aim only to get as much information as possible in the most efficient way available. But if we are concerned about human development, the people matter. Some ethical questions arise. "What may we and what may we not do in evaluating?", "What about the cultural dignity, values and privacy of the participants?", "Who really benefits from the whole exercise?"

These points can be expanded by the animator. After the introduction, participants are asked to discuss in small groups, "What should and should not be done in evaluation?" These points are then shared in the whole group.

## 7.  PLANNING QUESTIONS AND INDICATORS FOR SPECIFIC PROGRAMS

The next step is for people involved in the same programs, e.g. youth, women, literacy, etc., to take that program and do the following tasks.

### a.  Clarify aims

Clarify the original aims of that program; for example, the aim of a youth program might be to give skills to unemployed school leavers so they can begin self-employment projects.

### b. Form questions

After the major aims and short-term objectives have been clarified and written down, each aim and objective needs evaluation questions. The groups can go back to list the categories summarised in step 3.

After completing this task, two groups can be paired to give each an opportunity to review their work. The purpose of this sharing is for each group to help the other to clarify their questions and see if they are:

- simple,
- clear,
- meaningful, and
- have no gaps or missing points.

### c. Guidelines on deciding indicators

> **Evaluation can become very broad and thus meaningless if we do not have clear signs or indicators of change.**

For example, an objective might be "to get youth more involved". An evaluation question, "Are the youth more involved?", is much too general. What would be some indicators or signs, after a one-year program, which might show this has been achieved? Are there more youth on committees? How many? Do the youth give suggestions for programs? If so, are they accepted?

The groups now go back to work and try to decide on indicators for each of the categories or headings they have discussed.

When this task is completed, it is useful to have a whole group discussion on what they learnt about forming questions and choosing indicators. It is important to note that indicators need to be checked before they are generally accepted as true signs of change. For example, because a husband and wife now go to church together, it does not necessarily mean the marriage workshop has improved their marriage.

Forming questions and finding indicators is the work of the group that is preparing to conduct the evaluation. One would not usually ask village people to go through the whole process, though they are sometimes very good at suggesting signs which show things are getting better or getting worse.

## 8. METHODS OF EVALUATION

The whole group is asked to brainstorm different methods which can be used to carry out a process of evaluation. These are written on newsprint.

In groups of 4 or 5 discuss "What are the advantages and disadvantages of each method?"

This session is very important because people can learn a lot from each other about methods they might never have used in their own situation. Some methods that may be suggested are:

- written questionnaires
- informal/oral interviews
- structured interviews
- group discussion method
  in whole group or in small group
- observation
- survey
- case studies
- slides, photos or drawings

## 9. HISTORICAL REFLECTION WITH SLIDES, PHOTOS OR DRAWINGS

It can be very helpful to recall the history of a program to stimulate memory and critical reflection as the first step of evaluation. A series of photographs, drawings, or slides can be used for this.

In Brazil, this has been brilliantly done in the whole Pastoral program of the diocese of São Paulo. Cardinal Arns requested Paulo Freire and the cartoonist Claudius to design an evaluation process.

They took the theme of migration from rural to urban areas, which had been used as the theme for Lenten discussions in Basic Christian Communities throughout Brazil in 1980.

They prepared a slide show telling the story of a young migrant who has to leave the rural areas because of hunger, poverty and deprivation.

He arrives in São Paulo, finds a friend who tells him the story of the formation of their small Christian community, the popular movements to deal with the rising cost of living and low wages, and the strike of metal workers.

After each section, animators led the communities in critical reflection on the actions planned and taken. The last section deliberately raises a lot of unsolved problems and challenges the group to plan their program for the future.

Case studies and simple posters dealing with one key problem can also be used very effectively, with carefully chosen questions.

> **To try and to fail is not laziness**
> — Sierra Leone

And did you succeed, Joao?*
Well, we still have a lot of problems in front of us.

There are still a lot of people who believe that the priest by himself will solve everything.

There are a lot of pessimists who believe that the situation is hopeless and will never change.

---

\*     This series is from a slide called *"The Journey of a People"* prepared by the Pastoral Program of the Archdiocese of São Paulo, Brazil.

There are a lot of men who believe that a woman's place is in the home.

There are a lot of white people who think they are superior to blacks.

There are those who believe that the people are too weak to face the powerful.

And there are still those who let themselves be tricked by the smiles of those in power.

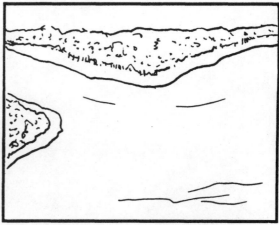

But in spite of all this, our groups do exist. They began weak and fragile, as a dew-drop that, drop by drop, began to form a little rivulet of water.

But if it joins with other streams, it turns into a river growing stronger and stronger till it turns into the sea.

## 10. PLANNING THE PROGRAM FOR PARTICIPATORY EVALUATION

The final step is to plan how the group will implement the participatory evaluation process.

Ask people to answer the following questions in project or interest groups:

a. What aspects of your program do you aim to evaluate?
For example, a literacy group might say it needs to evaluate on several levels:
i. every literacy class needs to evaluate its own program,
ii. all the materials need to be evaluated with some of the literacy participants,
iii. the effectiveness of each teacher needs to be assessed, etc.

b. What method will you use for each of the aims you have mentioned? What indicators and what questions are important to include?

c. Who will do what, when and where? Make out a time, place and person chart to indicate your plan.

d. All plans are shared in the whole group.

The last step of a participatory evaluation workshop is to have an evaluation of the workshop itself. Look out! The level of critical awareness will have gone up during this process, but it will be a healthy sign!

# B. Evaluation exercises for workshops

It is extremely important, if a program is to meet the needs of the group and continue to improve, that there be evaluations. These can at the midpoint of a workshop and at the end of a workshop. The following exercises are some ways of doing this.

## 1. SIMPLE AND RELIABLE

The simplest form of evaluation gives all participants an opportunity to respond to three basic questions:

a. What has been most helpful so far?
b. What has not been helpful so far?
c. What suggestions do you have for the next time?

These questions can be answered either in writing or discussion (first in small groups and then a whole group discussion).

**Time**     If in writing only, this takes about 15 – 20 minutes. If in discussion, 45 minutes to 1 hour.

**Materials**  Pencils, paper, newsprint, tape, felt pens.

**Note:**    A summary of all points should be written on newsprint during or after this session and presented at the beginning of the following session. The suggestions made by participants should be reflected in the ongoing program that the animators have prepared.

## 2. ONE WORD OR FEELINGS

This is a quick method of taking the "temperature" of the group, and getting in touch with any dissatisfactions.

**Procedure**

a. Each person is asked to write down one or two words expressing how they feel about the program so far.
b. The animator goes round the circle asking each person to say only the one or two words they wrote. Do not start discussion until all have given their words.
c. The animator asks some, especially those who have expressed dissatisfaction or whose comments are puzzling, to explain why they said what they did.

**Time**     About 30 minutes, unless some major dissatisfaction is expressed. Then it is very important to explore the causes of it thoroughly.

**Materials**  Pencils, if necessary.

## 3.  LISTING THE MAIN PARTS OF THE PROGRAM

This method of evaluation is more thorough.

**Procedure**

a.  Hand out a typed copy of the important elements of the program or write a list of them on newsprint.

b.  Each person is asked to write whether that part of the program was:
- very helpful
- fairly helpful
- not helpful

They are also asked to write a remark about each part. If an opportunity is provided to discuss with participants why they rated each item as they did, one often gets a much fuller understanding of people's needs, and good ideas for the future.

**Time**    About 45 minutes to 1 hour.

**Materials**  Duplicated copies of each part of the workshop (or listed on newsprint), paper and pencils.


## 4.  WHY DO WE DO WHAT WE DO?

Many times during the workshop, participants ask the planning team, why are we doing this or that? This is often a genuine interest in group methods and the philosophy of education. Their questions should not be taken lightly or defensively. Much of the theory behind these methods is found in previous chapters. However, each of us needs to be able to explain this theory in a simple and straightforward way.

In groups of three, take one question at a time. One person is asked the first question by the other two persons. That person must try to explain the answer to the satisfaction of the other two people. When finished, go onto the next question and the next person answers that one. Rotate around the group until you have finished making a note of any questions you cannot answer and ask the whole group at the end of the exercise.

**Questions**

1.  Why do we have introductions at the beginning of a workshop?
2.  Why do we ask people to introduce a partner rather than themselves?
3.  Why do we use name tags which are so big?
4.  Why do we ask participants what they expect of the workshop?
5.  Why do we ask people to discuss in groups of 3s?
6.  Why do we ask people to discuss in groups of 6s rather than groups of 3s sometimes?
7.  Why do we invite participants to come in teams rather than as isolated individuals?
8.  Why do we have a team to staff a workshop rather than doing it by ourselves?
9.  When do you as a facilitator join participants in their discussions and when do you not join them?
10. Why do we ask people to find others they do not know well at the beginning of a workshop to discuss a topic?

11. Why do we put the chairs in a circle?
12. Why do we brainstorm some topics and not others?
13. Why do we stop discussions and have people "buzz" or talk with their neighbour?
14. Why do we use newsprint? When is it helpful and when is it not helpful to use newsprint?
15. Why do we use codes? Simulation games?
16. Why do we have a listening exercise?
17. Why do we have participants evaluate the workshops at the middle and at the end?
18. Why do we ask people to plan in groups which are from the same area?
19. Why do we ask the teams to share their plans with the whole group?
20. Why do we have discussions on the situation of the poor and the displaced in our society?
21. Why do we have discussions on the influence of the economically rich in our society?

---

**Learn from mistakes**

"What we learn we do, and when we do, we see what is wrong. So we learn also from our mistakes and achievements. The mistakes show where there are shortcomings in our knowledge, weak points which have to be eliminated. This means that it is in the process of producing that we correct our mistakes . . .

"Practice is not enough. One must also know, study. Without practice, without being combined with force, intelligence remains sterile. Without intelligence, without knowledge, force remains blind, a brute force . . . Study is like a lamp in the night which shows us the way. To work without study is to advance in the dark. One can go forward, of course, but at great risk of stumbling or taking the wrong path."

*The African Liberation Reader,*
Zed Press, London, 1982, Vol. 1, pp. 116-117.
From a paper by Samora Machel, 1971.